Trevin Wax is an insightful thinker and skilled writer. In *Rethink Your Self* he shows that following our own dreams and desires won't work; we must look to God to learn who we are and are meant to be. Nothing less can bring us purpose and delight.

Randy Alcorn, author of *Happiness* and *Heaven*

Trevin is a gift to church, and his book reflects this reality. In *Rethink Your Self*, you are going to discover your true self—self created in the image and likeness of a God who cares for us and cultivates our character to reach its redemptive potential.

Dr. Derwin L. Gray, lead pastor, Transformation Church; author of *The Good Life: What Jesus Teaches About Finding True Happiness*

The common advice to "be yourself" is easier given than taken. In the modern age, shaping our identities and orienting our lives is more complicated than at any time in human history. With clarity, knowledge, and wisdom, Trevin Wax explains the unique challenges this particular cultural moment presents us in being ourselves, and places these challenges into the context of an eternal design—one that can equip each of us to be who God created and called us to be.

Karen Swallow Prior, author of *On Reading Well: Finding the Good Life through Great Books* and *Fierce Convictions: The Extraordinary Life of Hannah More—Poet, Reformer, Abolitionist*

Rethink Your Self is a guide for people who long to soar in life. Trevin Wax exposes unproductive frames of mind, tackles big questions, and sorts out the complexity of the human heart in amazingly clear prose. Highly recommended!

René Breuel, author of *The Paradox of Happiness*

We live in a society that is obsessed with identity and yet filled with people who have no idea who they are. In this book, Trevin Wax gently persuasively questions the common sense of our day of "being true to yourself" and points to the paradoxical beauty of denying yourself and following Jesus. In a culture that says "look within," we would do well to follow Trevin Wax's advice to look up.

Jeremy Treat, PhD, pastor for Preaching and Vision at Reality LA; author of *Seek First* and *The Crucified King*

RETHINK YOUR SELF

RETHINK YOUR SELF

TREVIN WAX THE POWER OF LOOKING UP
BEFORE LOOKING IN

B&H
PUBLISHING
NASHVILLE, TENNESSEE

For Timothy, Julia, and David

May you be renewed in knowledge
according to the image of your Creator.
Colossians 3:10

Contents

Introduction

This is not a self-help book.

If you're looking for tips and strategies to improve yourself and feel fulfilled, you can find plenty of books with commonsense wisdom geared toward that end. This is not one of them.

My goal isn't to help you *help* yourself, but to help you *rethink* yourself. And the only way you will rethink yourself is if, before rushing too quickly to commonsense answers, you encounter a different set of questions. The first step in rethinking yourself is when you decide not to accept so easily the most common answers to the most commonly asked questions.

One of the best places to see what passes for common sense is the graduation ceremony—commencement services where young people stride across the platform, celebrate their achievements, and toss their caps as they step into a world brimming with possibilities. You're probably familiar with the inspiring words you hear at these events, even though you can't remember the specifics because, unless they were out of the ordinary, they offered up the usual commonsensical fare about the future:

> *Follow your heart.*
> *Chase your dreams.*
> *You are enough.*
> *You do you.*
> *No matter what, be true to yourself.*

If you were to discern a main point from graduation ceremonies across the United States, you'd come up with something like this: *the purpose of life is to discover yourself by looking deep down, and then express yourself to the world, no matter what anyone else—family members, friends, colleagues, previous generations, or religious institutions—might say.*

Common sense, right?

If you're going to rethink yourself, you'll have to question those slogans and the ideas behind them. You'll need to stop assuming that the world works the way you've always thought it should work, or that your purpose is whatever you've assumed it to be, or that your road to happiness must follow the well-tread paths of everyone else.

A warning: rethinking yourself means first re-*thinking,* and rethinking can be unsettling. It requires you to put things on the table that you've never thought to examine. It means probing your inner motivations and the desires of your heart in ways that may bother you and upset your priorities. It means coming face-to-face with some of your deepest fears and anxieties. It will open your eyes to things you've taken for granted while making you doubt things you've considered to be basic truths about the world. Rethinking yourself means more than just looking inward to your heart; it requires you to see yourself in relation to the world in a different way.

Rethinking yourself also means rethinking your *self.* It means figuring out what it is that makes you *you.* How do you discover who you are—what constitutes the core of your being? What is a "self" anyway, and what makes your "self" different from everyone else?

I assume you're not reading this book because you want me to tell you everything you want to hear, or because you want me to reaffirm everything you already believe to be true. With a title like *Rethink Your Self,* you've probably picked up this book for one of two reasons.

The first is that you may be facing some important decisions and you want to get them right. You want to be the best version of yourself you can be, and you want to fulfill whatever calling you feel is most important in your life. But you know how easy it is to fail to reach your potential, or to fail to discern your purpose in life, and the big decisions down the road frighten you a little (or maybe, a lot!). You want to be authentic and to make choices that align with the deepest part of yourself, but you wonder if the commonsense wisdom you hear everywhere else is adequate in equipping you to find and follow the best path in life.

The second reason you may be interested in this book is because you're on the other side of some decisions you've made in the past, and as you look back at your life, you feel the weight of more than a few regrets. You've always gone along with what passes for common sense (*be yourself, follow your heart, chase your dreams*), but it hasn't led to the happiness you expected to experience by now. You're anxious. You're irritable. You worry you're missing out on something better. It looks like everyone else has found the secret to the good life, while you're just muddling through the day trying to keep up appearances. In fact, you wonder if you'll ever get what you want out of life. In bleaker moments, you wonder if you even *know* what you want out of life. On the other side of life throwing you some curveballs, you're not sure you even know what it means to "be yourself" anymore.

Whether you're the first reader or the second, the point is that you're ready for self-examination. You sense the need to take a step back, look at your life, take stock of things, and get a fresh perspective on your identity and purpose. You're ready to examine things you've always taken for granted, and you're wondering if what passes for common sense really makes sense.

If that's you, you've already taken the first step to rethinking yourself. The world needs more people who ask questions no one else thinks about, who doubt the ideas everyone else assumes to be true, and who are courageous enough to become unsettled and uncomfortable in challenging their once-cherished beliefs. It takes guts to put yourself on the table and invite scrutiny about who you are and what your purpose is.

So, as we start our journey together, we're going to take a closer look at the usual way people in our society think of themselves. We'll see what works and what doesn't in this framework for thinking about our purpose. Next, we'll consider another way of seeing ourselves—what passes for common sense in other cultures and societies. Then, we will consider how the ancient wisdom of the Bible describes our purpose in life and how this perspective challenges the commonsense wisdom of our day.

Even if you don't consider yourself religious or spiritual, I hope you'll be open-minded toward that ancient perspective. There's wisdom to be found there, and it has stood the test of time. Let's get started.

CHAPTER 1

Looking In, Around, and Up

There's something exhilarating about being told you can be whatever you want to be. With enough hard work and determination, you can achieve anything! You are free to discover your identity and purpose and then display yourself for the world to see.

It's no wonder that self-help books and feel-good movies and some of the biggest pop songs rely on this message of inspiration. We love stories of people who overcome the odds, who remain true to themselves no matter the obstacles, and who succeed in life at being whatever they set out to be. *You can do whatever you want!* There's something exhilarating in that message of freedom.

But the message of freedom delivered to someone in their teens sounds different when directed to someone in their fifties. Once you chase your dreams for a few years, experience some of life's big setbacks, and regret some decisions that didn't get you where you thought you wanted to go, you may hear that inspiring talk a little differently. It sounds more exhausting than exhilarating. Instead of making you feel good about yourself and your future, it makes you feel bad about yourself and worse about what may lie ahead.

Just think what the message implies: if you're not where you want to be in life, something must be wrong . . . *with you*. After all, if anyone can achieve anything and you've not yet reached the pinnacle of your success or the fulfillment of your dreams, then you've failed somehow. It's all on you.

How do you deal with such disappointment? Some people choose to see themselves as a victim of circumstances. *The world is out to get me, everything is rigged to keep me from being myself, and there's no point in pursuing happiness anymore. Everything has conspired against me.* Other people blame themselves. *I'm just not good enough. I can't keep up. Maybe everyone else is doing better than me because, deep down, everyone else is better than me.* Bitterness and resentment fill the heart of the first person; guilt and anxiety, the second.

In both cases, discouragement sets in because none of the cheery promises came true. If you alone are responsible for finding yourself and fulfilling your purpose, and if it's within your grasp to become and do whatever you set your heart to, and you've not succeeded, what else can you conclude except that you're a victim because the world has wronged you, or you're a failure because you've not overcome the obstacles to your happiness? Whether you failed to overcome the odds or failed to find happiness, the point is *you* failed. Life beat you up. You lost.

At this point, the commonsense response in our society is to double down on the original promise. *Time to get back up and try again! Your disappointment and failure is just one more obstacle to overcome. You can achieve anything you want and reach your dreams if you refuse to give up.* But what if returning to the promises that disappointed you just sets you up for bigger failures and more discouragement in the future? What will it take before we ask if the original message was even true?

Here is where we need to step back and take a closer look at the way most of us see the world. Before we can *re*think anything, we need a clearer vision of how we think without thinking. Most of what we assume to be true about our lives is unconscious. We gravitate toward a certain way of understanding the world without ever calling it into question.

We don't always know why we're inclined to make certain choices, because our view of life isn't something we consider all the time. We don't wake up every morning wondering about the meaning of life, or our deepest source of identity, or what our purpose is. We get up, eat some breakfast, brush our teeth, and get dressed for school or work or whatever we've got going on that day.

Your life is formed as much by what you *unconsciously* assume is the purpose of life as it is by any book you've read or talk you've listened to on the matter. That's why, in order to re*think* your self, you've first got to *think* about yourself.

Why does everyone just nod along to the idea that the purpose of life is to "be true to yourself" and "chase your dreams" and "follow your heart," as if the message is so obviously true that it would be silly to question it? Because most people in our society view themselves and the world like this: you look *in*, then *around*, and then *up*. The default setting for people in our society is to figure out life according to these priorities. In, around, and up. In other words, we first look inside ourselves, then look around to others, and then (usually, but not always) look up to God or some higher power. Look in, around, and then up.

Look In

The "look in" approach to life means that your purpose is to look inside yourself in order to discover who you truly are—to find what makes you unique—and then to take hold of your authentic self and emerge with it intact and uncompromised. Who are you? Only you can figure out the answer, and the way you find out is by looking deep into your heart to discover your uniqueness, to come to terms with what you want most from life.

To "look in" means you first look inside for the answers to life's biggest questions. Another way to describe this orientation to life is through what I call the four D's: definition, desires, display, and design.

Definition

Definition refers to the way you define yourself. Who are you? What are you? What is your identity? What is your purpose in life? We must decide the answers to these questions for ourselves—or so we're told. The way to find fulfillment in life is to look inside yourself as an individual and determine what is unique about you—who you are deep down. You are responsible for defining yourself. No one else can do this for you. It's a deeply personal act. *You do you. Be true to yourself. Be you.* You define your identity.

Desires

Defining yourself may not be as easy as it sounds. How can you know if you are defining yourself authentically? Here is where *desires* come in. Defining yourself requires you to get in touch with the deepest desires of your heart. You must dig below the surface until you unearth the answer to what you really want most out of life. Who do you want to be? What do you want to accomplish? What will it take for you to be happy? What are the desires that drive you? It's only when you discover your deepest desires that you can be assured of your identity and purpose in life. Until you know your desires, you can't truly follow your heart or chase your dreams. Your desires determine your destiny.

Display

Once you've discovered your desires and defined your identity accordingly, it's time to put yourself on display. You're ready for the world to see who you really are. Now you *look around* to find people who will celebrate what it is that makes you unique. You look for people to affirm who you are and what you want out of life. You gather friends who cheer you on in your quest to follow your heart.

It's never been easier to express yourself now that we all have opportunities online to develop a persona through what we write, what we wear, what pictures we post, or how we present ourselves. People care deeply about their public image not because they're just faking it or trying to impress people, but because their self-expression is so tightly connected to their self-definition. At least at some unconscious level, we connect affirmation to personhood. To not affirm someone's true self is, in some sense, to deny their personhood—which, in the scheme we've been following, means to not affirm someone's *desires* is to not affirm their *identity*.

We look *in* to discover our desires and define ourselves, and then we look *around* for people who support our quest for authenticity.

Design

Definition, desires, display, and finally *design*. As you go through life, you find yourself changing, and whenever your desires shift, the image you want to put on display for other people may shift too. You may reach a point where you feel inauthentic, like you've been putting on a show for people and aren't truly expressing the essence of who you are. Or maybe you feel insecure because people don't seem to like the person you've presented, and you want to get in touch with yourself at a deeper level and see if others will accept a more attractive version of yourself. Or maybe you once felt special and unique but now you see that you're a lot like everyone else and you don't really stand out.

What happens next is a process of redesign. You reinvent yourself. You see yourself in need of an upgrade. When you experience a period of self-stagnation where you worry about failing to reach your greatest potential, you begin a process of reinvention by looking deep within yourself once more until you come up with a new design—a new *you* to be true to.

We used to make jokes about the "design" phase by calling it a mid-life crisis, but nowadays it can happen to anyone at any time. Tired of your old self? Try on a new image! Artists and musicians do this in order to stay relevant—to maintain the element of surprise for their fans, or perhaps to gain some new ones. But now that most of us have become broadcasters of our lives online, we feel similar pressure. Redesign your life. Reinvent yourself.

Looking In Before Looking Up

Those are the four D's, and they demonstrate the "look in" approach to life—the priority of looking *in* to find ourselves and desires, and then looking *around* to express our identity to others. But many people find that only looking *in* and *around* is unsatisfying. They believe something is missing—a spiritual dimension to their life. They long for something transcendent, and so they look *up*. They look for ways to incorporate that deep spiritual longing or religious impulse into their lives.

What does this look like in practice? You add a spiritual dimension to your life through adopting certain exercises, such as meditation, or fasting, or prayer, or attending a religious service, or a certain kind of exercise and dieting regimen intended to rid your body of toxins. The "look in" approach to life isn't opposed to spirituality; it borrows spiritual practices that help you get better at looking inside your heart. People often sense the need to get in touch with their spiritual side, and so after they've looked *in* to discover who they are, and after they've looked *around* to gain the support and approval of others, they look *up* to a higher power to provide a spiritual dimension to life.

In, around, and up. For most people in our society, this is the set of priorities that gives shape to how we view our purpose and identity. Sociologists and researchers have done studies that show the prevalence of this way of thinking in North America—where the purpose of life is to be true to yourself, to find happiness, and to be a good person. It transcends many cultural and political divides. It is the default way of thinking for young people, even across different religious groups.[1]

Despite the differences in our religious views or political affiliations or geographical location, there's a common thread throughout our society: the purpose of life is to *look in* (first and foremost), *look around* (for support and affirmation), and then *look up* (for inspiration). That's how it works. You define yourself, pursue your desires, put yourself on display for others to see, and then occasionally, when necessary, design a new *you* as you move through life.[2]

Put your own life under the magnifying glass for a moment. Is this approach to life true of you? How do you make decisions? How do you determine what you want from life? Where do you turn when you're in trouble? What do you expect your friends to do for you? How do you define yourself and grow in authenticity? What do you expect out of your faith tradition or your relationship with God?

If you're like most people in our society, you discover your purpose by looking in, around, and up. Not surprisingly, then, it's just common sense for people to say you've got to be true to yourself, be real and authentic, follow your dreams, and express your uniqueness.

Such a deeply personal journey, isn't it? That's why it's going to be difficult to put it on the examining table. But the process of *rethinking* yourself requires us to ask some tough questions. Does the "look in" approach actually work? Does it give the happiness and satisfaction it promises? Does it make for a healthy society? We are living through an era of increased polarization politically and culturally. Is it possible that the "look in" way of life is one of the causes? Does this way of thinking bring us together or drive us apart?

Consider how we handle disagreements or criticism. When someone questions your choices in life, you get defensive, don't you? Especially when you've done the hard work of looking deep within yourself to discover who you are and what you want out of life. The moment someone questions your values or beliefs about yourself and the world, you're likely to receive that challenge as a personal attack. No wonder it gets harder to have dialogue in society!

When people look inside themselves in order to define their purpose, and then look around in order to receive support for their decisions, they find it hard to receive criticism of any kind. Criticism makes us feel condemned, as if someone has called into question our deepest desires or the contribution of our uniqueness to the world. Not only does it feel like people are critiquing our actions, it feels like they are condemning our very identity.

The problem is, our values and beliefs do not always align with others, and theirs don't align with us either. And so we feel trapped. On the one hand, if we're going to be true to ourselves, we ought to be able to say whatever we think about anything. On the other hand, if we question or critique someone else, we know we may be hindering their attempt to be true to themselves. What a strange cultural bind! We're supposed to express ourselves, but only so long as we never call into question someone else's self-expression.

As you're starting to see, there are some issues that arise in societies where the "look in" approach is widespread. We'll explore other problems in more detail later on, but first we need to be reminded that what passes for common sense in our society isn't common sense everywhere. There are alternatives. Throughout history, most societies have not seen the world this way at all. If you're going to rethink yourself, you should be acquainted with the way people in other parts of the world think of themselves. And for many, looking *in* first leads to loneliness and societal disintegration. According to these cultures, we should start by looking *around*.

Reflection Questions

How do you deal with disappointment, when things don't turn out the way you hoped?

In what ways does the "look in" approach describe your overall outlook on life? In what ways is your outlook different?

Have you ever gone through a "redesign" where you tried to reinvent yourself in some way?

CHAPTER 2

Looking Around, Up, and In

For most of the people who have graced this earth in centuries past, the option of thinking about life in the way described in the last chapter—looking in, around, and up—would not have made sense. It would have seemed strange to tell my wife's grandparents, who grew up in a village in Romania, "You can be anything you want to be," because there were so few choices available to them. They tried to make the most of their circumstances, and they worked the land to support themselves and their family. Going off on your own into the wilderness to discover yourself before coming back and expecting everyone to get in line with your newfound identity was nearly unthinkable for them. It's not that there weren't opportunities for contemplation in their generation, but they did not have the luxury of choosing between multiple options when it came to identity and purpose. Life was too hard for individuals to prioritize journeys of self-discovery. That's why, for many people in the past and for many people around the world today, the approach to life is not to look *in*, *around*, and *up*, but to look *around*, *up*, and then *in*. When defining and discovering purpose, the community takes precedent over the individual.

Look Around

The reason it's important to take a closer look at cultures where people look *around* before they look *in* is not because it's necessarily better or worse, but so that we recognize that what passes as common sense in our society—that we are in charge of our destiny and our self-definition—is not common sense to everybody everywhere else. It certainly wasn't common sense for most of the people who lived and died in the centuries before us, and it's still not common sense for some people in many parts of the world today.

For us, discovering purpose is an individual quest. You start with yourself and look inside to find who you are and what you want from life. But throughout history and around the world today, discovering purpose is a community exercise. You start with the people around you, and it's in community that you discover who you are. Instead of *you* telling the *community* who you are, the *community* tells *you* who you are. You look around *first*. So let's look again at the four D's from the last chapter and see how they work in cultures where common sense follows the "look around" approach.

Definition

As we saw earlier, common sense in our society is that you take the lead in defining yourself by discovering your uniqueness. But in other societies, you discover who you are by looking to what the people around you say about you. You discover your identity not by looking inside as a lone individual ("I"), but by considering who you are in relation to your family or tribe ("We"). Your self is defined and formed primarily by social ties and expectations.

According to the "look around" approach, you find out who you are by who you belong to. For example, consider your vocation. Consider my wife's Romanian grandparents again. Like most people around them, their "jobs" were determined not by personal passion or individual interest, but by heritage. If your father was a blacksmith, you were likely to be a blacksmith. A son's life looked a lot like his father's. A daughter's life looked much like her mother's. The community, through the passing of each generation, would slowly change over time, but people largely accepted their stations in life and made the best of whatever circumstances they inherited.

You didn't define yourself on your own; you accepted the definition pressed upon you by your family, your clan, or your tribe. You discovered yourself by looking *around* first, not *in*.

Desires

What about your deepest desires? In the "look around" approach, what *you* want most from life comes after whatever the community wants most from life. The only way for groups of people to survive and flourish together is for individual desires to be subsumed under the community's deepest needs. Unless you prioritize the most crucial needs of the community, you never find the freedom to pursue some of your personal desires.

A good example of this is found in arranged marriages. Throughout history, marriage has been as much an economic and social arrangement as a romantic one, which is why a young man and woman's personal desires were usually not the main consideration. That's not to say romantic love never flourished between husbands and wives (sometimes heartfelt passion developed over time if it didn't exist at the beginning), and it's not to say that romance was never involved at the start. The point is, the family's needs have often taken precedence over the individual's desires. You looked around before you looked in.

Although most of us resist the thought of our job or marriage being decided for us by someone else, there's something in this way of life that we recognize as noble. The Christmas classic *It's a Wonderful Life* may be a favorite for many Americans who take the "look in" approach to life, but it also appeals to aspects of the "look around" mentality. The main character, George Bailey, wants nothing more than to leave the dumpy little office where his father has labored, to "shake the dust of this crummy little town off [his] feet" and "see the world!" But again and again, the desires of his family and the needs of his community keep him from escaping Bedford Falls. When he looks inside, he sees frustrated dreams. When he looks around, he sees people who need him.

The story captures the tension of what constitutes the good life: to prioritize looking *in* or looking *around*. And by the film's end, George Bailey is forced to look *up*, when through the help of an angel he discovers that "no man is a failure who has friends." Even in a culture like ours, where looking *in* is common sense, we find something noble and heroic in stories that celebrate looking *around*.

Display

Self-expression and self-display take on a different purpose in societies that prioritize looking *around*. Whereas in our culture, you gather friends and join communities that affirm and support the way you define yourself, the "look around" approach finds it less important that the community conform to you, and more important that you show how you conform to the community. Your self-display is a signal of your commitment to others.

Even in a society dominated by the "look in" approach, we find pockets of the "look around" mentality. Tribal markers that become part of a person's self-display show up in small religious sects or in gangs that serve as "street families" for disadvantaged youth. The goal is to prove to the world that you belong, that you know your proper place, and that you will fulfill whatever role is best for the community. In the "look in" approach, we define ourselves by how we stand out; in the "look around" approach, we define ourselves by how we fit in and build up the world to which we belong.

Design

Just as we've seen a community understanding of definition, desires, and display, the same is true of design.

In many societies, the idea that someone would reinvent themselves or embrace a new design for their life seems out of place and perhaps even self-absorbed and egotistical. If there is a reshaping of definition, it happens for the whole community, not just for individuals. Reforming and redesigning yourself is something that everyone takes on together as a project; it's not an individual effort.

You may wonder if or how looking *up* has any place in this approach to life. Sometimes, looking up is how this kind of community confirms its rituals and self-understanding. It's the appeal to a sacred order that gives eternal significance to the choices of the community. Looking up reinforces and confirms whatever is already accepted as common sense. For this reason, you may find strict prohibitions regarding certain foods or taboos around certain words or actions. Looking up may include the veneration of one's ancestors, where the link between present and past generations is strengthened by the idea that not only can you displease the community in the present, but also your forefathers and mothers from the past. Looking up is how present habits and rituals stay connected to the sacred order that keeps society stable.

To sum up, then, the purpose of life is this: you look *around* to the community in order to discover who you are, you look *up* and see how the community's way of life is connected to a higher design for the way the world is supposed to work, and then you look *in* and do the hard work of bringing yourself into conformity with others' expectations for you as you take your proper place in the world.

The Positives and Problems

The "look around" approach to life may feel foreign to you. It doesn't fit with our society's favorite songs and anthems about breaking free from others' expectations. It doesn't make sense in the story lines of many of our favorite films, where the main character is a hero because he or she refuses to conform to someone else's vision for their life. Although we have exceptions here and there, we rarely think of the hero who strengthens the bonds and fulfills the needs of the community.

But if we look carefully, we can see the reasons why so many people see this approach to life as full of wisdom. It's true that someone else may be responsible for establishing the path that you're obligated to walk down, but think about how much stress disappears when you don't have to forge your own way through the world. You may not feel as "free" to choose from dozens or hundreds of options, but you benefit from a sense of stability and security (not to mention freedom from anxiety over making the right choice all the time!).

Furthermore, there's something beautiful in the notion that you can only make sense of yourself within the context of a community, where your focus is less on your own identity and more on the rich relationships that will sustain you in love during the hardest times. We often romanticize the notion of the lone hero forging a new way in the world—in opposition to family or community expectations—without considering the downside: loneliness and isolation. There are trade-offs in life. You may love the idea of "determining your own path no matter what!" but others may find more satisfaction in community bonds that provide a deep sense of belonging.

Now, just as there are problems with the "look in" approach (which we will see in greater detail in the following chapters), so also there are problems with societies that adopt the "look around" approach. In fact, you could say that the enthusiasm we have for looking *in* is often a reaction to the view that tells us to look *around*.

The "look around" way of thinking may offer benefits, but it's not without its drawbacks. A stifling conformity can descend upon these cultures, where the expectations become unbearable and the shame of stepping out of line can crush the individual. It's one thing to feel like a personal failure, but it's another to feel like you've failed your entire community—all the people you look around to and respect. In extreme cases, the shame of letting others down can lead to self-harm, even suicide.

A fatalistic acceptance of injustice will sometimes mark societies that focus on looking around over looking in. Fate leads to a quiet acceptance of your identity and your purpose in life based on whatever roles others give you. If you find yourself without the basic necessities of life, or suffer under the weight of community expectations that enshrine inequality as a sacred fact, the feeling of fate can become overpowering. The dignity of the individual can get crushed by societal forces.

Even the spiritual aspects common to this way of life can feel oppressive, where ancient codes and rituals can take precedent over individual needs. The emphasis on conformity can create a culture in which no one feels incentivized to improve the lot of the least fortunate.

We won't spend more time on the commonsense assumptions of other societies—the "look around" approach—because the way you see the world is likely more in line with what I described in the previous chapter. You look in, around, and then up. But I hope that taking this brief journey into other societies has served an important purpose: to show you that our "commonsense" assumptions when it comes to purpose and identity aren't actually common sense, because most of the world, past and present, sees these things differently! One of the steps to rethinking yourself is to question some of your cherished notions and unmask your hidden assumptions, and I hope the revelation that only a minority of people think this way has helped you do that.

After reading about the "look around" approach, you may think: *Maybe the "look in" approach isn't so bad after all. If forced to decide between looking in first versus looking around first, I'll stick with looking in.* That's understandable. One of the best things about traveling is that you often come to appreciate your home a little more. But there are problems with common sense back home, too. That's why our next step will be to return to the "look in" approach and examine some issues you may never have noticed before.

Reflection Questions

In what ways does the "look around" approach to life resonate with you? What parts of this outlook on life do you resist?

What are some groups you've belonged to in the past? How did the group influence your perception of yourself?

How is the "look around" approach to life different from the "look in" approach?

CHAPTER 3

The Challenges of Defining Yourself

L et's return to what passes for common sense in our society today: the point of life is to look *in* and discover who you are by figuring out your deepest desires, then look *around* in order to display your newfound self to others who will affirm and support you, and finally look *up* to something spiritual that might add meaning to your life. Look in, look around, and look up.

Of course, we can't forget that, as we saw in the previous chapter, all across the world and over the course of many centuries, most people have had a different understanding. They believed it was just plain common sense that you'd look *around* first, and then *up*, and (maybe) *in*. Perhaps that's why, once upon a time, the "look in" approach to life we're now used to felt revolutionary and rebellious—especially when it went against the traditional way of life, where the individual is defined in relation to the community. Our society was formed, in part, through rebelling against the ways in which the community might shackle you and your impulses. How exciting to be an individual, free and unique, as opposed to just disappearing into the crowd! Why not break free from cultural expectations and generational demands?

Yet for many today, the "look in" approach has lost some of its luster. Its promises often go unfulfilled. If you feel the need to rethink yourself, it's probably because you feel uneasy and unsure about the commonsense wisdom out there. Maybe you're young and you wonder if it will truly deliver the happiness it promises. Or maybe you're older and you wonder why your pursuits have left you empty instead of fulfilled.

You may have grown to love certain aspects of this way of life—the excitement of considering many options, the thrill of discovering how you are wired, or the joy of feeling like you've made a unique contribution through something you've created or value you've added to a group. To be sure, there are positive elements to the "look in, around, and up" framework. If there were no benefits, it wouldn't be so widespread. But along with the positives come negatives. Along with the benefits come drawbacks. And the older and wiser you get, the larger the negative aspects loom over your life. My goal in this chapter and the next is to return to the four D's to show how the initial thrill of the "look in" approach fades over time and sets us up for disappointment.

The Challenges of Self-Definition

Recent studies show that 91 percent of Americans agree with this statement: "The best way to find yourself is by looking within yourself."[3] It's hard to find a more widespread affirmation of the "look in" approach than that! In other words, if you want to discover who you are and what your purpose is, the place to look is inside your heart. You look inside for the answers. Trust your heart. Go with your gut. No one else gets to define you.

The freedom you feel when you see your life this way can be mesmerizing. You get to determine your destiny. You are free to define yourself however you want. If you want to change your name and start over, go for it. You can define yourself by your career or your hobby or your talents. You and you alone are the ultimate determiner of who you are and how you express yourself. You alone possess intimate knowledge of what makes you unique, and you alone can determine how to bring that sense of specialness out for the world.

Best of all, when you look inside to define yourself, whatever you find there is good. Whatever you find is beautiful. No one gets to tell you your self-definition is wrong or bad or ugly. Defining yourself is the ultimate adventure.

But there is a downside to this way of thinking: the whole project depends on you. What happens when you try to determine your destiny but everything falls apart? What do you do when you chase dreams but never reach them? Is failure fatal to your purpose and identity? Does failure threaten your sense of self?

Even more, what if defining yourself in isolation, or in opposition to what others may think about your life, feels adventurous at first but over time leads to loneliness? What happens when you miss out on the satisfying sense that you've contributed something significant to your community? Wouldn't making a contribution to a community be more fulfilling than just gathering people around you who will applaud however you define yourself?

The whole project of looking inside to find yourself is filled with contradictions. Let's consider one of the biggest problems: is it possible to discover your uniqueness without comparing yourself to other people? Can you really prioritize looking *in* over looking *around?*

Consider a man who defines himself by his career as a teacher. He has a knack for explaining things, he likes his students, and he finds satisfaction and a sense of worth in his work. When you talk with him and ask why he teaches the way he does, he tells you about two teachers who had an impact on his life when he was young. The first teacher was excellent—guiding his students through the course and stirring up in them a hunger and thirst for learning. The second teacher was horrible—lording his authority over the class in ways that stifled creativity and led to disdain for the subject. Naturally, he wants to imitate the good teacher, and he wants to avoid anything that resembles the method of the bad teacher.

We could say that this young man has looked deep within himself to discover his passions and gifts and that he has, all by himself, arrived at the conclusion that he should define his identity and purpose through his career as a teacher. But did he actually do this on his own, in isolation? No. He is following a path that the good teacher laid out for him, and he is reacting to the negative effects of the bad teacher's methods. In the end, the young teacher may think he is looking inside and charting his own path, but both the good and bad teachers he had in the past are still highly influential in his self-definition. He wants to be like one and unlike the other. He isn't truly alone, looking within to find himself.

"But," you may say, "I'm not trying to be like anyone else I know. I'm different than everyone else—on purpose." Maybe. Maybe in this case you would be like a young man who only had horrible teachers. Year after year he had to deal with different kinds of problems with his teachers: mocking and abuse of authority and laziness and poor explanatory skills. So, the young man says, "I'm going to be a good teacher, different than all those horrible teachers I've had." But don't you see—he's still not defining himself in isolation. He's still looking around in order to define himself, even if he's doing so over and against every teacher he's ever had.

The "look in" approach to life imagines that our individuality is pitted against the community, as if the community always threatens to stifle us or squeeze us into conformity. And so, we assume that the way to discover and define ourselves is to sequester our deepest self, and to dismiss our background, the influence of our family, or whomever we admire or despise in the community around us.

But this isolated plan for discovering yourself is impossible. It's a myth. Try as you may, you cannot discover and define yourself without reference to other people. It won't work. And the irony is, when you feel the most free—when you are the most dedicated to standing out and being different than others, you are *still* defining yourself in response and reaction to others. Even the choice to cast off certain expectations or restraints from your community is an action taken in reference to other people. It's not possible to find yourself merely by looking inside yourself. Looking *in* and looking *around* are just too intertwined.

What's more, no matter how much you try to be a certain kind of person, to live according to the definition you've set for yourself, you find yourself slipping into patterns and habits that you don't want to be true of you. What if the man who wants to be like the good teacher finds himself, in his worst moments of exhaustion and burnout, resembling the bad teacher? How many of us claim we will never do certain things our parents did, only to find to our dismay that escaping the influential patterns set by them is more difficult than we ever imagined?

When we fail to live up to the definition we've set for ourselves, we're caught in another dilemma. Are you most truly yourself in your best moments, when you are living up to the ideal? Or are you most truly yourself in your worst moments, when the "real you" that comes out in your words and actions frightens and disappoints you? Is the real you the person you want to become, or is it the person you are right now?

The Deceptions of Desire

As you can see, looking inside to define yourself turns out to be more complicated than we thought. The more we think about it, the more we realize that who we are is always in flux, and it's hard to define your identity and find your purpose when your self is always changing. These complications show up again when we consider what it means to discover and pursue our deepest longings. Our desires aren't static.

A recent survey shows 86 percent of Americans, when asked about finding happiness, agree with the statement: "To be fulfilled in life, you should pursue the things you desire most."[4] Here is the key to happiness! Look inside to find yourself, figure out what you desire most, and then find fulfillment in life by pursuing those desires. Go for whatever you want, and never give up!

But two major problems hinder our discovery and pursuit of our deepest desires. First, it's not as easy as you think to figure out what you really want out of life. It's too simplistic to think you'll find fulfillment by chasing what you want the most, because it's not always easy to figure out what you want the most. Second, the deeper you dig into your heart, the more you'll find desires that don't align. Sometimes you want things that come into conflict with each other.

Let's start with the first problem. How do you come to understand what you really want out of life? People often think that looking into your heart to figure out your desires is the easy part; it's the pursuit of happiness—of fulfilling your deepest desires—that takes so much energy. But that's simply not the case. The truth is, you don't know what will make you happy.

Haven't you heard about people who chased long and hard after a dream, who ran with single-minded passion to fulfill a deep desire, only to discover a surprising sense of emptiness after they'd reached their goal? People who went after fame or fortune or recognition or pleasure and succeeded in getting whatever it was they wanted— they'll tell you that it didn't bring happiness. They're still unfulfilled. Why do we think it would be different for us? The truth is, we may think we know what we want, that we've discovered our deepest desire, only to find out later, when we get it, that we must have really wanted something else all along.

Then there's the flipside to the same problem. You may convince yourself that you *don't* have a particular desire, only to find yourself later in life longing for whatever it is you never wanted.

Imagine a man and woman who get married. They say their deepest desire is for companionship and freedom. They want to enjoy each other's company as they travel the world, pursue their individual careers, and maintain maximum flexibility in their plans. Kids don't fit into this picture because having children would force them to settle down and accept certain constraints on their time, and would hinder their flexibility. What if, later in life, they regret aspects of their decision to forgo having children? They wonder how their life might have been different, how their marriage might have been different, or what the inconveniences and restricted freedom that comes from parenting might have done for their character. What if, at the end of their life, they look back and find themselves with a desire they didn't know they had? Did they get what they really wanted, or did their desires deceive them?

Consider another example. What if someone's deep desire is to be seen as successful? The overachiever wants to add more accomplishments to his résumé. He wakes up every morning with the dream of creating story after story of success. For years, in chasing that desire, his health suffers. His family is neglected. He pursues that desire with total determination, overcoming any obstacle in his way, and at the end of life, what if he looks back with pride at the wins he's racked up, but finds himself unsatisfied? What if the success he thought he wanted most lets him down, and he is suddenly struck by another desire—to be known and loved by his family?

Looking into your heart to discover your deepest desires isn't as easy as you think it is. Your desires will trick you. "Follow your heart," we say, but we can find case after case where people say their hearts led them astray.

This isn't new. More than 1,600 years ago, the theologian Gregory of Nyssa pointed out the problem: "For as soon as a man satisfies his desire by obtaining what he wants, he starts to desire something else and finds himself empty again; and if he satisfies his desire with this, he becomes empty once again and ready for still another."[5]

That's what brings us to the second problem with the notion that the way to be fulfilled in life is to pursue whatever you desire the most. *Your desires don't always align.* They come into conflict. You want to be the wealthiest and most successful person in the office, and yet you also want plenty of leisure time to spend with your family. You want to eat whatever you want whenever you want, but you also want to enjoy good health for many years to come. You want the freedom and independence that come with money and time, and yet you also want the closeness and love of raising children.

We live in a world that says, *Pursue whatever you desire the most! You can have it all.* But you can't. The world doesn't work that way.

I remember a professor in graduate school telling us on the first day that it may be morally wrong for some of us to get an A in his class. What he meant was this: the demands we would have to meet in order to get an A would require a sacrifice of time that might be better spent in service to our family or in fulfilling other responsibilities. He encouraged us to be satisfied with getting a B if it meant we were keeping our priorities straight. Years later, that counsel still reminds me that it's impossible to fully escape certain limitations in life. You are not infinite. You have limits. Choosing one path means forsaking all others. Everyone does away with certain desires; the question is, which desires should die, and which ones should live?

It can be stressful to think that choosing one desire means rejecting another. How do you know if you're making the right decision? We love the idea that we have endless choices before us. It sounds so exciting! But eventually, the normal limits of life will press in. Our choices will become more constrained. We'll be forced to make certain decisions, and if we don't—if we try to delay our decisions in order to prolong what some describe as a period in which "no dreams have been permanently dashed, no doors have been permanently closed, every possibility for happiness is still alive"[6]—we will succumb to paralysis. Not choosing is itself a choice. Pursuing one desire will require you to say no to another. As *New York Times* columnist David Brooks writes:

> If you aren't saying a permanent no to anything, giving anything up, then you probably aren't diving into anything fully. A life of commitment means saying a thousand noes for the sake of a few precious yeses.[7]

Everything in us resists closing a door on our future, but without closing one door, we can never truly walk through another.

Then there's the question of good and bad desires. We have seen that the "look in" approach tells us to look into our hearts, discover our desires, and pursue them. But what if, looking into your heart, you discover a desire that you are ready to pursue with single-minded devotion, but the desire is harmful to someone else? What if the desire is bad for you, too? Talk to someone who has struggled with addiction and they'll tell you that some of the strongest desires you can feel are the worst desires to pursue. You might say, "Well, of course, addiction is bad." But aren't we conditioned to assume that *any* desire we find within ourselves is good? Who gets to determine whether a desire is good or bad?

Common sense today says that we alone can determine what is right or wrong for ourselves,[8] and that being true to ourselves means we must break free from constraints and outdated moral codes. But what if fulfilling our desires would cause us to trample on others? What if other people are hurt by our pursuit of whatever we want the most? And what if your deepest desires turn you into a monstrous person, and, like Gollum in *The Lord of the Rings,* the object you desire the most poisons your mind and shrivels your soul?

It's here we must raise the question: *Do desires define who you are, or do they reveal who you are?*

If your desires define you, then you have no option but to submit to them. After all, anything less would be forfeiting your identity. On the other hand, if your desires reveal you, then you have the option to refine them. You can use them as a mirror that shows you your heart, and you can respond by reforming and reshaping them in a way that is best for you and others.

Many people today assume that our desires define us. They are masters; we are servants. When we discover a desire, we see it as integral to our identity, and we think that to deny or question or repress it would be to deny ourselves and become inauthentic.

But what if our desires are not as reliable as we think they are? What if we should instead interrogate our desires, asking, "Is this good or bad for me, for others, for the world? Should I follow this desire, or should I suppress it?" Everyone may say you should listen to your heart, but sometimes your heart lies. Sometimes you don't know what you really want. Sometimes the things you want contradict each other. And sometimes the things you want would be harmful.

Defining yourself by your desires turns out to be more complicated than you might think. What's more, you often find you need other people to help you discover what you want the most. How many of us have found we need a mentor or someone with wisdom to ask us difficult questions, to probe our motivations, or to point us away from desires that hurt us and toward desires that are truly good for us? Looking *in* to define ourselves by our desires turns out to be impossible. We can't help but look around, too. That's why we feel the need to express ourselves and to put our selves on display. But the "look in" approach to life leads to challenges with our self-display also, as we'll see in the next chapter.

Reflection Questions

What failures have you experienced in your life? How have those experiences affected the way you see yourself?

How do you answer this question: "Is the real you the person you want to become, or is it the person you are right now?"

What is it like when your desires come into conflict with each other? When have you regretted chasing desires you thought you wanted most?

CHAPTER 4

The Challenges of Displaying Yourself

L ooking in without looking around isn't as easy as we might think. We're told that what matters most is whatever we think about ourselves, not what others say. But the truth is, we do care what others say, and even when we act like we don't, we're deliberately choosing a path contrary to others' opinions, which is a weird way of still being driven, to some extent, by someone else's viewpoint. We also know that we need each other. You can't be the best person you can be without someone from the outside being honest with you, showing you what you're really like rather than just what you think you're like.

The commonsense approach of "looking in" taking priority over everything else doesn't mean we never look around; it's just that looking around at others is supposed to be secondary. We're to discover who we are by getting in touch with our deepest desires, and once we emerge from that cocoon of self-reflection, we put ourselves on display for the world. Our goal is to gather around us people who appreciate the uniqueness we've discovered in ourselves, and who will affirm and support our quest for authenticity.

Displaying yourself doesn't take much effort these days. With the arrival of social media, you can start an account and begin to build a personal, public profile within minutes. It has never been easier to create and broadcast the image you want others to see. Most people like at least a little attention. We want to be liked. We want to be noticed. We want others to accept us as we are. Whenever we hear the critical voices of self-judgment in our head, we like knowing that others are saying or thinking nice things about us. And so we look for ways to create the kind of persona we want online. Some like the social competition for other people's attention and comments. Others like joining groups or playing games to try and be the best. We share our progress in our fitness app, or when we reach a new goal in a popular game.

The point is, we're all broadcasters now, and we're all waiting for someone's applause.

It's hard to overestimate what this has done to the notion of friendship. In a world where looking in takes priority over looking around, when we eventually do look around, we've trained our hearts to gravitate toward people who will affirm the way we define ourselves and who will cheer us on as we put on display our true selves for all the world to see. We think that the most important thing we can do for the world is to bring out our unique-ness and express it for everyone else. Isn't it true, after all, that the world needs more people who refuse to conform to others' expectations? We need people who will stand out, who will draw outside the lines, and who will cheer on the rule-breakers, right?

In this kind of culture, the meaning and signifi-cance of friendship undergoes a major alteration. In ancient times, friendship meant mutual commitment and unabashed truth-telling. True friends would tell you the truth. Yes, they would remain committed to you no matter what you were going through or what others thought of you. But the truest of friends cared about your heart enough to confront you when you started down a path that was bad for you or bad for others. True friend-ship was about acceptance *and* aspiration—accepting you as you are (warts and all), but also calling out the best in what you could be.

Today, the aspirational side of friendship has slipped. Friendships that involve truth-telling falter fast. We are told that a true friend accepts you as you are and celebrates you as you are, full stop. True friends don't just accept your warts and flaws; they're supposed to celebrate them (or at least never mention them). A true friend supports whatever individual journey of self-discovery you may be on.

We expect total acceptance and affirmation from our friends these days. Because we broadcast so much of our lives so much of the time, and because cyberbullying and negativity and criticism run rampant in society, we feel we need the support of our friends to pick us back up and encourage and strengthen us. When you've faced harsh comments, experienced the meanness of people online or in person, or just had a rough day at work, the last thing you want is a critique from a "friend." You want unequivocal support. Total affirmation. Even if you're wrong about something, you want someone to tell you you're right. You want someone to tell you that even your flaws and failures are beautiful.[9]

Unfortunately, the "look in" approach to life weakens us and fails to prepare us for what we'll encounter in the real world. We expect to be affirmed in our uniqueness and are therefore shocked when others question or challenge us. And so we look around for friendships based on affirmation and support, even if what we really need are people who will tell us the truth about ourselves. We turn to friends who will coddle us, and that process of coddling makes us less capable of dealing with criticism in the real world.[10] We feel more fragile than ever because our friendships are built upon flattery, not reality. Ironically, the more we are flattered, the more fragile we become. The thing we expect to build us up is the very thing that makes us so easy to tear down.

It's funny, but many people think that in a "look in" culture everyone should just naturally become more accepting of each other's quest to find and express themselves. But that's not what happens. Our self-displays are in conflict with each other. One person's life choices will call into question another's, because all of us, despite our intentions, are indicating by our choices what we think is *the best way to live*. Our expressions are never merely individualistic. The moment we look around to others, the moment we feel our own choices are called into question, and the moment others see how we choose to live, they may question their own choices as well.

Add to this atmosphere the pressure that comes about in a world where we're supposed to believe in equality (we are fundamentally the same deep down) but also in uniqueness (we are all special), and we run into a strange contradiction. On the one hand, we're all equal, so no one should stand out. On the other hand, we're all unique, so everyone should stand out all the time. Obviously, this won't work. The result is a lonely world where everyone is individually trying to figure out who they are and what they want to be, where we don't have as many true friends, while our feeds are filled with superficial friends.

The aspirational side to friendship begins to fade, and with it a real sense of commitment. Our friendships become shallower because our commitments are thin. We don't want to be tied down or have too many obligations. True friendship might impinge upon our time, demanding that we sacrifice our own freedom and pursuit of fulfillment in order to help someone else. And so we prefer looser attachments that won't drag us down.

Our friendships also become shallower because they get reduced to constant praise of someone's self-display and self-expression. Friendships have degenerated into the "thumbs up" sign on a social media platform. As we've seen, it's hard to imagine a friend having your best interest at heart if they challenge you, because that would mean questioning the deeply personal work you've done in figuring out who you are, what you want, and how you've presented yourself to the world.

Strangely enough, here's an example where our desire for friendship and support doesn't actually line up with what we *really* want. We say we want friends who will affirm us just as we are and not challenge us or question our self-definition. But when our friends do that—from a distance, rarely committed to us in any substantive way—all their comments and thumbs-up signs become less significant. The praise doesn't satisfy us. We stop believing it. Because our friends don't tell us the truth about ourselves when it hurts, we stop trusting that they're telling the truth about us when it feels good. We drown in showers of praise.

Here is how *New York* Magazine columnist Heather Havrilesky describes the effect of social media on young people who write her for advice:

> No matter how hard you try, someone else out there is taking the same raw ingredients and making a better life out of them. And the curated version of *you* that lives online also feels hopelessly polished and inaccurate—and you feel, somehow, that you alone are the inauthentic one.[11]

The world is awash in superficial compliments, and rather than making us all feel good about ourselves, we begin to question whether or not we're truly understood and loved. We feel like the person we're portraying in public or online isn't the "real me," and all the likes in the world ring hollow because our friends are expressing their approval for an avatar, not a real person. Or we feel like the person we're portraying *is* the real me, but the likes still don't satisfy because we don't feel close enough or committed enough to invite someone to say what they really think.

Do you see the conflict? We yearn to become better, to grow, and to get feedback from others. In other words, *we do* want to be judged. We want to get better. But at the same time, we want to be affirmed. We want to stay the same. We want to be declared "good" just as we are, but we also want to be called to something better.[12] And when these desires run up against each other, our friendships fail, and after a while, some people—rather than display themselves—decide to disappear.

Redesigning Your Self

The relentless quest for both self-acceptance and self-perfection leads some people to retreat and consider starting over. It's time for a new design. The "look in" approach to life offers many ways of talking about this effort to go back into yourself, figure out what it is you *really* want, and bring that out to the world again. I call it the "redesign" phase.

You see this reinvention in the entertainment industry with stars who change up their image in order to remain relevant. In some cases, it may be that the famous person doesn't know anymore who he is, and so he tries on different personas much like he'd give a performance, trying to figure out what fits. In other cases, perhaps the celebrity felt she was more authentic in the past, but over time came to doubt the flattery from all her fans and so adopted a new design—a different persona—to see if her followers would still accept and love her.

You don't have to be a movie star or celebrity to be drawn by the desire to have a new start or develop a new public image. In an age of social media where we constantly broadcast the details of our lives, it's easier and feels more natural to try to redesign yourself than ever before. And that's what many do. After growing frustrated with the person we've presented to the world, we may retreat for a time, or disappear from online inter-action, not so we can stay forever hidden from the eyes of others, but so we can change costumes or rework our image. We consider ways we might redesign our lives, our look, our way of being in the world. We used to call this a midlife crisis, but nowadays it can happen every few years. In the adolescent stages, it seems like it can happen even more frequently.

This longing for newness—to have a new name, a new image, a new reputation—drives us deeper and deeper inside ourselves, but all the digging begins to wear us out and wear us down. Just as we felt overly flattered or overly criticized for the person we put on display before, we wonder if we will feel the same after unveiling our new self. The doubts and self-criticisms mount in our hearts, and we wonder if we're really being authentic or if we're sacrificing the path to reaching our fullest potential. The endless self-analysis can make us feel like our phone or computer when there are too many apps or windows open; it's best to just shut down and restart (or look for an upgrade).

The commonsense wisdom of the world says, *Do it again.* Go through the process again. Distressed and disappointed with yourself? Well, don't wallow in guilt and anxiety. Just take another good, long look inside to discover your deepest desires, find a better way to define yourself, then display your individuality for the world to see and affirm. The cycle continues. We emerge with a "new and improved" self, and we go through the same anxiety-ridden process of seeing how others respond.

Looking Up

The problems with the "look in" approach to life seem to be multiplying, don't they? You sense the areas of anxiety and wonder how to escape the exhaustion. This is the point where many people attempt one last effort to make the "look in" approach work: looking up. It may come last in terms of priority (in, around, *then* up), but it's still an option. Does looking up resolve the tension? Let's see how it plays out.

The desire for a spiritual dimension in life, something that feels transcendent and contributes to our sense of wholeness and wellness, is strong for many people. Surveys show that even people who do not believe in God still find themselves praying from time to time. Likewise, people who claim no religious affiliation often borrow rituals and practices from different religions in order to discover a deeper connection to the world or to a higher power.[13]

But what if this way of looking up is still just another way of looking in? After all, aren't you really just looking up for help in your own process of defining and displaying yourself? Or looking up to claim divine approval?

Looking up, when it comes last in terms of priority, is more about finding a "God" who will get behind your personal project of being true to yourself. And that creates the same problem we ran into when "looking around" follows "looking in"—friendships grow shallower and connections dissolve, except this time, the shallowness and superficiality involve God.

When you think the purpose of life is to find your deepest self and express that to the world, then all of your most significant relationships are recast in light of self-fulfillment. Marriage is about finding your "soul mate," someone who completes you and makes you happy as you pursue and become the best version of whatever makes you unique. Friendship becomes an avenue for mutual self-fulfillment, where it's easy to take on new friendships or leave behind old ones based on their success in offering personal benefits. Religion (the decision to look *up* after you've looked in and around) may add a spiritual dimension to your life, but it's the life you've already defined for yourself. Sure, you may go to church or join a religious group, but you see your faith community much the way a consumer sees a club or a gym: it exists to provide you with religious services and spiritual feelings. The teachings and activities are only relevant so long as they better your way of life.

Some people have claimed that the "look in" approach to life leads away from religion. I don't think that's necessarily the case. Plenty of people still want to look up, even if it comes last in terms of priority.

The end result of the "look in" approach to life isn't the emptying of churches, but the filling of churches with people who believe they need spiritual assistance in being true to themselves. Religious practices don't disappear; they morph into something adaptable and helpful.

Religion becomes less about shared beliefs and values and more about uniting people who all embrace faith on their own terms. The idea of a faith based on something real, enduring, objective, and true (for everyone, not just yourself) doesn't make much sense in this kind of world. Faith becomes a subjective thing, a feeling that serves as an aid in your pursuit of self-expression and self-fulfillment.

The "look in" approach to life still maintains a place for "looking up," but what you're looking for is divine affirmation and assistance in your life as you've determined it. You're looking for inspiration intended to lift you up and restore your sense of self so you can continue down the path you've chosen. If you belong to a church, your inspiration will come from biblical sources—words of encouragement or exhortation, or psalms of lament or prophecies of restoration. But divorced from their historical setting or divested of their biblical context, even biblical words no longer have the power to *truly* challenge you about the path you may be on. They are marshaled in support of the path you've already chosen.[14]

In other words, church attendance, devotional books, religious practices—all of these become ways of helping you along in the life you envision for yourself (a life of seeking to find and express who you are), rather than powerful words that might radically reorient and shift your self-understanding. We can "mount up on wings like eagles," "run and not grow weary," "be strong and courageous," and find joy in "God's plans to prosper us" as we walk life's road. These words and images are drawn from the Bible, but they've been reduced to inspiration and shorn of any sharp edge of challenge. So yes, we look up, but only as long as our fundamental sense of self-definition and self-display go unchallenged.

But is this what it means to really look up? In the past, religion played a very different role. It didn't mean "pick and choose whichever religion you think will help you live your life as you define it." Even now, for most religious people in the world (outside of our society), it *still* doesn't mean that. It's no wonder that devout Christians or Muslims or Hindus or Jews—those who believe their religious faith says something true about the world, regardless of how "helpful" it is—protest the appropriation of certain religious practices without any kind of serious commitment. It's like trying to enjoy all the benefits of a religious identity without adopting the authentic version, because the authentic version would challenge you.

It may feel authentic to "look up" in this way, but in doing so, you choose personal authenticity over an authentic religious tradition. The self takes center stage. Even God must get in line.

A Better Way?

In this chapter and the last, we've seen several positive elements to the "look in" approach to life. Looking in, around, and up reminds us of the uniqueness and dignity of every individual, and it calls us to discover a particular gift we can offer to the world and the people around us. There's something fundamentally right in the desire to reach our potential and receive the approval of other people. The longing for a new name, a new face, a new persona, taps into something nearly universal. We want to be made new.

But we've also seen how this approach to life comes with plenty of problems. It doesn't lead to the happiness it promises. We can do our best to keep tweaking this approach, to try and figure out better ways to follow the set of priorities of looking *in*, *around*, and then *up*. Or we can throw up our hands and say, *Let's see if there's a better way to go about this!*

Thankfully, there is. But in order to understand this better way, we'll have to take a closer look at something authentic: the ancient wisdom we find in the story of our world as told by the Bible. Unlike our society, which starts by looking in, and unlike other societies that start by looking around, the Bible inverts both commonsense ways of thinking. We look up *first*. And strangely, it is through this counterintuitive approach that we find our truest selves.

Reflection Questions

How would you define "friendship"? Is your view more about acceptance or aspiration?

What are some ways you've sought affirmation from people around you?

What role does spirituality play in your search to be true to yourself? What does it mean to be "authentic" when it comes to religion?

CHAPTER 5

Look Up

Up until now, we've looked at two approaches to life that pass for common sense in the world. In some parts of the world, you look *around* first to your closest community or family, then *up* to a sacred order that covers all things, and then *in*. The purpose of life is to find happiness through fulfilling your role alongside your family and your community.

For many in our society, you look *in* first in order to define who you are by discovering your deepest desires, then *around* at people who will support and affirm your choices in life, and then *up* to a higher power that adds a spiritual dimension to your journey.

The problem with these approaches is their starting points. Neither you nor others can bear the weight of your quest for happiness. When the community is the starting point, it can become oppressive in its demand for conformity. We seek the approval of others until we forget ourselves in the process. When you as an individual are the starting point, you find it hard not to collapse under the weight of all the expectations for happiness and success that you've placed on yourself. We don't know ourselves well enough to figure out what we really want, and even when we get what we thought we wanted, we find fulfillment to be elusive. What's more, when suffering invades our lives, we don't know how to handle it or how to respond.

Neither the community nor the individual can withstand the pressure of our pursuit of happiness. Looking in isn't the answer. Neither is looking around.

A Different Path

But what if there's another way? What if that way counters what our society imagines the purpose of life to be? What if, instead of starting by looking in, then around, then up, we start by looking up, then around, and in? What if we were to reverse the priorities and go at it from the other side? How would a "look up" approach change the way we define ourselves, and the way we determine our desires, and the way we display ourselves? How would reversing the order change the way we live?

Thankfully, this way exists. But it's too often left untried. Not because it's impossible, but because it's a challenge in a world where the default mode is to "look in." No matter how many problems you may see with the way of life we've considered in previous chapters, you will find it hard to resist it because so much of our culture draws us back toward that way of imagining the world.

Even if you're someone with strong family and community ties, you're still likely to start looking in before looking around due to cultural expectations. Even if you're spiritual or religious, with a strong sense of right and wrong, you're still likely to look up last, only after looking in and around. A different approach requires us to radically rethink our selves and our purpose in life. Not only will we have to rethink our identity, we'll also need to develop practices and habits to reinforce the new direction—looking *up*, *around*, and then *in*. Reversing the priority will be difficult because the commonsense approach is so ingrained in our minds and hearts.

The good news is you're reading this book because you feel up to the challenge of rethinking yourself. And it's here that I must be up front about how we will proceed. The "look up" approach to life is what we see when we read the Bible. The wisdom contained in these ancient books that tell the story of the world from the beginning of time (Genesis) to the end (Revelation) reveals an approach to life that differs from what passes for common sense today. What's more, the Bible's wisdom, however counterintuitive it may seem to us, lays out a path that intends to lead us to everlasting happiness.[15] The Bible is after your joy, not averse to it.

Perhaps you are familiar with the Bible, having read it as part of a literature class or having consulted it for some nuggets of inspiration or encouragement over the years. Maybe you are a regular churchgoer and a frequent reader of the Bible because you believe it to be God's Word and that it has all the answers you need to life. Maybe you grew up in a religious environment where it felt like all you got from the Bible was a stifling list of rules and regulations designed to press you into conformity. Or perhaps you're not familiar with the Bible at all, and you remain open to its message just like you'd be open to any number of religious texts that have helped people over the centuries.

Whatever the case, I hope you will approach the following chapters with an open mind. If your study of the Bible in the past has been primarily for inspiration, then you may be surprised by what you find here. (Frequent encounters with the Bible leave many people less with a feeling of inspiration and more with the impression that the *Bible* is what is inspired.) If you're a regular reader of the Bible, then my goal is to reveal areas of your heart and life that are more in line with "looking in" than "looking up." If your knowledge of the Bible has come through the context of a faith community where you felt oppressed and pushed down, as if the book was meant to shackle you and rob you of joy, then you may be surprised to find that the Bible challenges that kind of community and holds the keys to a different kind of freedom. And if you've never encountered the Bible before, I hope this next section of the book will be a worthy introduction to the world's best-selling book every year, and that it will lead you to study some of the Bible for yourself.

Design from Above

As I mentioned earlier, the Bible reverses the common-sense way so many of us approach life. Instead of giving priority to looking in, around, then up, the Bible would have us start by looking up, around, and then in.

In other words, from the start, the Bible demotes you. In terms of priority, you're not it. The story doesn't start with you.

It doesn't start with the people around you either—your family or community, as important as they may be. "In the beginning, God . . ."[16] These very first words of the Bible have us look up first because only God is strong enough to withstand the weight of all our hopes and dreams, fears and anxieties. Start with yourself, and you'll collapse. Start with community, and you'll conform. Start with God, and you'll come into your own by finding your truest self in relation to him. The "look up" approach to life starts with self-demotion. You're not at the center of the universe. The Bible holds that space for God.

That said, your self is not obliterated or suppressed. Even though the opening chapters of the Bible tell about the creation of the world and even though the focus is on a personal God who made all things, it soon becomes clear that human beings are supremely important in this world (and matter greatly to him). God didn't make the world out of obligation, but from love. We exist because we are loved. And even though it's true that God loves the whole world, the Bible claims that human beings stand apart from the rest of the creation, with dignity and worth that come from being made in God's image. There's something fundamentally right about the "look in" approach that celebrates our uniqueness. The "look up" approach doesn't deny that truth, but it refocuses and reprioritizes it, grounding our unique gifts and personalities in God, not in ourselves.

Being made in the image of God says something profound about our identity and purpose. We have worth and value because we reflect the God who made us; we have purpose because we were made to reflect him, like a mirror. In our work and rest, through our creativity and authority, in our relationship to others and to the world, we reflect the God who created us out of love.

To sum up, the beginning of the Bible starts with looking up before looking around or in. It starts with God. He's the point, not us. That means, ultimately, you're not self-creating; you're God-created. You're not self-defining; you're God-defined.

Right away, you may feel a twinge of resistance to this idea of being demoted. Look up first? Doesn't looking up imply the existence of something or someone above us? And doesn't belief in something or someone above us imply that we are accountable to an outside force? That we need to submit to someone else, and bring ourselves in line with some higher order and calling? The Bible's answer is *yes*. Absolutely.

The commonsense wisdom of today says that you are responsible for creating and designing yourself. You determine how you want to define and display yourself. You set the standard, you figure out what's right or wrong for you, and then you pursue your strongest desires, as long as you don't hurt anyone else. Whereas everyone assumes you're free to create yourself, design yourself, and define yourself, the Bible starts off by saying you're already created, designed, and defined. And yes, being created means there's a Creator. Being designed means there's a Designer. Being defined means there's a Definer.

That's the main reason why the "look up" approach is so challenging. It is radically and unapologetically God-centered. The Bible confronts a "me first" way of life with a "God first" world. The Bible confronts the "I" with the "I Am"—the name God gives himself as the creator and sustainer of life.[17] The world says we should look inward, while the Bible says to look upward.

There's something deep within us that both loves and hates this idea. We love the idea that we were created with the highest possible calling, with worth and value that comes from outside ourselves, and with a sense of the transcendent. There's joy that comes from knowing we did not create ourselves, that even before we were born we were known and loved by God. But we hate the idea that we'd be held accountable to a standard outside ourselves or that something above us has even more worth and value. We don't want to cede any authority in our lives to someone else.

In a "look in" world, the idea that we'd be required to conform to nature, or to a religious viewpoint, or to an outside source of morality feels constricting. You may feel like "looking up" is just another way of stifling "the real you" inside. When the Bible offers instruction about how to live, you may feel at first like you're betraying your own identity. If you submit to a truth that comes from outside yourself, are you somehow failing to "live your truth"?

We've been conditioned to accept the "look in" approach as the path of common sense. For this reason, when we first come into contact with the reality that God has claims on us, we shrink back. We feel like we're giving up our freedom. It feels more natural, more comfortable, to look in first, then around, and finally up. Looking up *after* you've looked in and around isn't so threatening. But looking up *first* gets in the way of our self-definition and self-fulfillment, and that's why we have an allergic reaction to it.

But the Bible rejects the kind of looking up that comes only after you've looked in and around. It demands that we look up first. Looking up last isn't really looking up at all. Why not? Because in the "look in" approach—when you are the one who defines who you are, and you are the one who finds people to affirm you as you are, and you are the one who decides to add a spiritual dimension to your life (such as God or a higher power or religious practice)—your relationship with God gets established on *your* terms. You're not adopting the authentic version of a religious faith; you're altering a religious faith in order to suit yourself. You may have a spiritual side, but you're living as if you're the ultimate authority in your life.

When looking up comes last, it just reinforces what you have already determined about yourself.

If there is a God and he really did make you and the rest of the world, then you don't get to define him in relation to you; he gets to define you in relation to him. And unless you look up first, you'll make God in your image rather than accept that you're made in his. You'll define God as you want him to be rather than discover God as he actually is.

The Selfish Impulse

If you find yourself initially shrinking back from the "look up" approach, don't be surprised. In a "look in" world, it feels intrusive and invasive to be confronted with a God who claims authority over you. But the Bible isn't shy about this truth. Neither do the authors of the Bible seem surprised that you'd react this way. Just a few chapters into the Bible's first book, we learn about human nature. There's a rebellious streak that runs through all of us. The Bible uses many words to describe this way of being bent or disordered, but the most dominant one is "sin."

"Sin" gets defined in many ways in our world. Some people use the word "sinful" as a synonym for a "delightful enticement." Other people think of "sin" as a personal failure, when you are pursuing an ideal and you fall short. Or perhaps it's when you break a rule or do something you feel guilty about later. Religious people tend to focus on a list of particular sins we should avoid (and then debate what should or shouldn't be on the list).

The Bible defines sin differently. At times, it's spoken of as a power—a supernatural force in the world that holds us captive. If you've ever felt like you were drawn irresistibly into doing something wrong, something you knew you'd regret, you've gotten a little taste of sin as a power. Sometimes, you don't feel like you're fully in charge. You do something you hate, or you say something you never wanted to say. In that moment, don't you feel like something powerful has taken hold of you? Like something outside you has led you to do something you wouldn't normally do? The Bible sometimes speaks of sin in this way—a malevolent and mysterious force of evil that can be terribly hard to resist.[18]

Other times, the Bible speaks of sin as a condition. Sin is something we do because we're marked by it. It's in our nature. The reason we have to teach little children not to lie, steal, and throw fits is because they tend to do these things even when they've not seen us model them.

When left to itself, unless we pull the steering wheel a certain way, a car naturally drifts. The same is true of the human heart. We drift toward attitudes and actions that are self-centered and self-absorbed. In this way, sin is a condition—the selfish bent of the human heart.

The Bible also speaks of sin as specific acts of wrong-doing. But it's not just that we break a rule here or there, but that in our rule-breaking, we are defying God. It's personal. It's not just disobeying a commandment of God, but also hurting the heart of God.

Sometimes, the Bible describes sin in terms of trying to demote God from being the one in charge of our lives. We put ourselves where God belongs. We call the shots. We imagine God revolving around us, instead of us revolving around God. Another word for this is idolatry—the making of an idol for ourselves. It's when we take something other than God and make it the most important part of our lives. Idolatry shows up in two ways: when you are ultimately dedicated and devoted to something (namely, yourself) other than God, and when you decide to define God as you'd like him to be rather than worship him for who he actually is.

The problem with sin (and idolatry) is that it hinders our pursuit of happiness in many ways. Our identity and purpose is to reflect God, but sin distorts the reflection. We still display God, but as a broken mirror, not a flawless one. Sin derails our best plans. It infects our best intentions. It robs joy from our greatest moments. It gnaws its way into our deepest desires. The result? Feelings of guilt and shame that can paralyze us in our pursuit of lasting fulfillment.

In the next chapters, we will see how the "look up" approach to life reconfigures and reimagines the four D's we saw in previous chapters: definition, desires, display, and design. But before we go there, let's review what we've just learned.

The "look up" approach starts off by demoting us (God is God and we are not) and then by diagnosing us (we're all infected by a disease that makes us selfish). We may not like the demotion. And we may not like the diagnosis. But the Bible isn't interested in giving us what we want as much as it's focused on giving us what we need. The good news is, we'll soon discover in the process of rethinking our selves that what we need most is ultimately what we want most, even if we don't know it.

Reflection Questions

Do you feel a sense of anticipation or something more like hesitation when considering the Bible's outlook on life? Why?

What is your reaction to the idea that you are to "look up" first, to a God who has designed you? Why do you have this reaction?

Where do you see the "selfish impulse" at work in your life?

CHAPTER 6

Our Original Purpose

Because the Bible turns upside down the normal script of looking *in*, *around*, and *up*, we can't start with how we define ourselves. We have to start with the fourth D and move our way backwards (or as the Bible would say, we've been looking at all of this backwards to begin with, and it's time to put things in the right order). So, we must begin with *design*.

In earlier chapters, we talked about ways in which people may—after a period of frustration in trying to define and display themselves—choose to redesign their lives and become a different kind of person. The Bible has much to say about that kind of redesign, too, but it comes later. First, it starts not with the person you would redesign yourself as, but the person that God designed you to be.

The Creator at the Center

One reason so many people have found the Bible to be well worth their time is because the Bible indicates all throughout its pages that there is meaning and purpose in life. There is meaning and purpose in suffering. There is meaning and purpose in all the setbacks and leaps forward, in all the events of history, and in all of your personal choices in your own life journey. The Bible takes a cosmic view of things and says there's a God who created the world.

On the surface, that's not an unpopular belief in our society. Plenty of people—the overwhelming majority, in fact—agree that there is a higher power, some sort of God who made the world.[19] Whether or not creation happened quickly or over time or through evolutionary processes (these are debates that still go on in many pockets of our society), surveys show that most people, regardless of what church affiliation they have or whether they are agnostic, believe that there is a powerful Being of some kind who made the world.

But they also believe that this God isn't too involved in our day-to-day lives. He's there to rely on in case you need help.[20] You can pray to him. He may answer; he may not. He's not overly interested in all the details of your life and how you live, but he's there to help you in the time of trouble. For this reason, some of the most popular passages in the Bible are read at funerals or weddings or in times of trouble—because they show God as this kind of cosmic helper who is there for us when we need him.

Make no mistake, the Bible does portray God as a helper in times of trouble, a rock, a fortress, someone you can hold on to when life gets crazy and there doesn't seem to be any relief. But that's not *all* the Bible says about God. If you remember earlier when we looked at the priority for most people (where looking *up* comes last), we saw that when people do look for a spiritual dimension, they want a higher power or a relationship with God that will give additional meaning and significance to life *as they have already defined it*. God isn't necessary, but he's helpful. If you need him, he's there. You can rely on him if you're in need, and you can benefit from the spiritual side of life if you want more purpose and meaning, but if you're okay on your own, that's fine too.

Starting with looking *up* changes the picture completely. Yes, God is a helper in times of need, but he's not some sort of cosmic bellhop ready to swoop down and comfort you whenever you need him, while otherwise remaining uninvolved in your life. That's not the picture we get from the Bible. The Bible leaves no doubt that God is at the blazing center of all things, like the sun, and we're revolving around him (like the planets). He's at the center. He's the very definition of perfection. He's holy (a word that means he is utterly unique, set apart, different from anything else). And he's the very meaning of love.

So, it's not about inventing the kind of spiritual being that we imagine would best support the kind of life we want to live. It's about recognizing that there is a powerful and personal God who created the world, who loves what he has created, and who has designed things to work a certain way.

The Grand Design

Design matters for anything we make, doesn't it? You can take a car to a junkyard and get money for scrap metal and for spare parts, but at that point, the car won't be running anymore. Its purpose has shifted from its original intention. It has become a hunk of metal, slowly rusting.

One of the first questions you ask about any invention (just ask the patent office of the United States) is, *What is it for?* What's the point, the purpose, the ideal for which this *thing*—whatever it is—exists?

The ancient philosophers were obsessed with this question. And they didn't just ask it about things; they asked it about *humans.* Socrates, Plato, Aristotle—these guys spent a lot of time talking about what it means to be a human being. They talked about ideals, about virtues and vices, about what makes you *more* human or what makes you *less* human—that is, what makes you more or less ideal. If there's not some sort of goal, some sort of vision of what a human being is supposed to be, how do you know if you're succeeding? If something is created and designed to work a certain way, unless you know what the purpose of the design is, you won't know if it's working.

Now, again, you might respond, "That's exactly the thing I am against. I don't believe in the notion that there is some ideal form of being a human; I want to be *authentic.*" This brings us to two ways of considering authenticity. What does it really mean to be "true to yourself"?

On the one hand, we're told we are most true to ourselves when we are pursuing whatever it is we want to do, when we are pursuing our desires. On the other hand, we're told that being true to yourself means looking at your life as a kind of project, figuring out what the *best* version of yourself would be, and then pursuing *that.* In a recent book, a thirty-something woman describes her "happiness project" and quickly discovers that her goal of "being herself" runs into a problem. There's *herself* as she currently is, and then there's *herself* as she would like to be. Which one is it?[21]

The ancient response to this question was to take the second route. What are you *for*? What defines the good life for a human? What makes you *more* of yourself, not *less*? A fork can feel like a spoon and try to become something different, but it's not going to be very useful when eating soup. The point is that you're authentic not whenever you're simply doing whatever you want to do, but what you were made to do. True authenticity is not about designing your own purpose in life, but instead discovering a purpose that makes sense based on the world we live in. You're looking for a purpose, a goal that fits both you and the world. And that makes the question of "design" unavoidable.

Not surprisingly, the Bible starts with design, too, and it says that humans were created with a specific purpose. You can succeed or fail at being who you are meant to be. This is one of the reasons why so many books about becoming the best version of yourself resonate so strongly with so many people. We strive for something. We are strivers, deep down. We want to fulfill our purpose in life. We may not know exactly what our purpose is, but we want to define it for ourselves and then run after it, to realize ourselves in some way.[22]

The Bible affirms that sense of striving but doesn't tell you to define your purpose in life by looking inside yourself. Instead, you discover your purpose by looking up to God. It's a process of *discovery*, not a process of *definition*—at least not at the start.

There are two ways that design works. There's a general design that exists not only for you as a person, but for all of humanity. It's true of everyone. The second is that you are designed individually, as someone who has a unique contribution to make to the world. There's a specific design that exists for you.

In our day, we rush to the second element of design, believing that we are unique and special and that we need to discover the essence of who we are and what we bring to the world. We consider the first element of design only secondarily, if at all. In fact, sometimes we pursue the second over and against the first—*I am unique and special and there is nothing about me that's true of everyone else.*

But the Bible doesn't start with the specific element. It says you should back up and start with what you share with all human beings everywhere. You should start by seeing what you as a human share with other humans. Only after you've done the hard work in understanding what it means to be *human* can you figure out what it means to be *you*.

Becoming a Display

Let's look a little closer at what the Bible says we were made for, in this general sense. Here we begin to move from design backwards to the next D—display.

The Bible isn't interested as much as we are in displaying ourselves for others to see. Its focus is that we would be a display of the image of God, that we would reflect the God who made us. This is the general understanding that unites all human beings and gives us a kind of uniqueness among all other creatures on earth. A tree may be designed to bear fruit, a squirrel may be designed to collect acorns, the sun may be designed to shine, but humans are designed to be a display for God. We bear his image. This is the purpose for which we were created—to praise the one who made us and to reflect his glory and power and character.

It doesn't matter who you are or where you came from or what you imagine your unique purpose in life to be. If you're human, the Bible says, you share this element of purpose with everyone else. You're designed to reflect God.

The way you do this is not just by religious exercises like going to church and singing songs. You are to reflect God in all the parts of your life: in the way you relate to other people, in the way you exercise authority in the sphere of life where you have influence, in the way you work with all your heart to make something of the world, in the way you rest from your labors. You reflect God in all of your life, not just through activities that fall into a "spiritual" category. But the point is that you are called to reflect him. You exist for his glory, to give him praise.

Right away, you may be resisting this idea, and for good reason. Doesn't this make God out to be some sort of praise-hungry monster? Why would God care so much about us reflecting him or making him look good? Doesn't this make him egotistical? That he has created the whole world to be always praising and worshiping him? Many in our day balk at this description of God.

The reason it rubs us the wrong way is that, once again, we're used to starting with looking *in* at ourselves, as if we are at the center of the universe. We like the idea of a spiritual being who's there *for us* much more than imagining that we exist *for him*. We like the idea of a God who makes us look better; we don't like the idea that we're here to make *him* look better.

Original Desires

This brings us to the next D: desires. Let's review for a moment. God has designed us in his image. The display that matters most for all human beings is how we fulfill our purpose in reflecting him. You may not like the idea that God wants our lives to revolve around him, and I understand why you'd feel that way, so that's why we need to see what the Bible says about our desires.

When you're in the world of the Bible, you quickly realize that God's desire for our praise and our individual desires as human beings *are not at their root in conflict*. They complement each other. Because God made us in his image to bring him glory, our deepest desire is *to worship*. Our deepest desire—common to every human being—is to love and be loved.

We should not imagine God as a harsh taskmaster up in the sky raining down judgment in lightning and thunderbolts and demanding we worship him because he's such an egotist. The picture the Bible paints is of a God who designed us to find our fullest happiness and satisfaction in knowing and loving him. When he calls us to praise him and to give him glory and to put him at the center of our lives, it's not because he cares about himself and not us—it's because he knows what will make us ultimately and eternally happy. After all, no one knows the design better than the Designer; God designed us and he knows what will satisfy us, and he wants us to experience that satisfaction in him.

Don't think of God as a distant authority figure scowling at you, but as a Father who knows that the place you'll feel the happiest is in the strength of his warm embrace. Or see him as the lover who woos you with good things, kindnesses in this world that you don't deserve but enjoy every day, telling you that you are the apple of his eye. This is a love relationship we're talking about, not a tyrant who fails to give any thought to the happiness of his subjects.

One of the most brilliant crystallizations of the Bible's teaching comes in a simple question and answer: *What is the chief end of man?* (Which means, what is the ultimate purpose or goal of a human being?). The answer is: *To glorify God and enjoy him forever.* Do you see the picture here? We were made not for grudging obedience to God without relationship, but to *enjoy* him. This implies that we are to know him. Our joy is part of the picture. Our ultimate happiness is at stake.

Here is where desires come in. Our deepest desires don't have to be unearthed in some sort of self-focused project. They are revealed in the Bible. Our deepest desire is to love and be loved, to know and be known, and to give ourselves totally in love to another. All our human relationships reflect dimly this desire; ultimately, only God can satisfy it.

The problem we face is that our desires are not always pure and good. We'll come back to this in the next chapter when we see what has gone wrong and how sin not only affects our design and display, but our desires, too. So many of the things we chase in life become objects of our worship. We want to worship. We want to give ourselves fully to something. And so we will serve something. Something will master us. We will be a slave to something. The question is, to what?

Defining Yourself

All of this brings us to the final D: *definition,* who you are. This is perhaps the most fundamental point to be made about how the Bible sees the human being. In the commonsense way we think of life, you are responsible for looking deep within yourself to define who you are and what your purpose is. No one can do this for you. You have to define yourself. In the commonsense way of life for other cultures, you are responsible to look around to the community in order to find out who you are and what your purpose is. You let the community define you. But in the Bible's view of things, *God defines who you are deep down.* You don't define yourself;

you discover the self that God has already defined. You receive a definition; you don't invent it.

At first, you may feel like this idea puts you in chains. *Wait? You mean I'm going to lose the freedom to define who I am? I don't want to give that up! I want to take responsibility for my life and decide who I'm going to be. I don't let anyone—not my neighbors, not my family, not my church, and certainly not some higher power or ancient book—tell me who I am or what I am going to do.* That's an understandable reaction in a world where common sense means you make your own way in life and you decide who and what you will be.

But what if the freedom we think we experience in defining ourselves is actually another kind of slavery? And what if submitting to someone else's definition of our life is actually the most freeing thing in the world? It seems impossible at first because we associate freedom with independence. But what if there is a deeper and more satisfying freedom? Like the freedom of a train as it speeds along the tracks laid for it, following its designated path to a destination. When you adopt the tracks God has laid for you—the definition he assigns you—*no one can take that away,* whereas a definition you have to determine for yourself, or a definition given you by others, could wind up being always in a state of flux. If you define yourself, you're a slave to your own ideas and desires. If the community defines you, you're a slave to the ideas and desires of others. But if God defines you, you're a slave to him, but you experience that slavery as freedom, because in adopting his definition *you are who you really were meant to be.* (I told you the Bible would be countercultural!)

We're going to see how the Bible flips the script in upcoming chapters, but first, we need to dig a little deeper into why we have these allergic reactions to the idea of God defining us, or being a display of God's glory. Why are we allergic to that kind of thinking? Until we can tamp down on the symptoms of an allergic reaction, we can't move forward. So next, we need to see why the "look in" approach to the world is so natural to us that, even with its problems, we'd rather stick with looking *in* instead of start with looking *up*.

Reflection Questions

Do you find yourself looking to God primarily as a helper for the life you've chosen for yourself? Or as the one who gives meaning and significance to your life? Why?

How would you define "the good life" for a human being? What were you made for?

How do you define "freedom"? How does your definition resemble or differ from the idea of freedom as described by the Bible?

CHAPTER 7

Our Unavoidable Flaw

When you start a journey of improving yourself—through an exercise regimen, a plan for healthier eating, or going to a counselor to work through various issues—you need an accurate assessment of your present state before you can move forward. If you decide you want to run a full marathon, you'll first need to grapple with the reality that you can hardly run a 5K without passing out (or throwing up!).

The same is true here. In order to rethink yourself, you need a better look at your current state. What kind of self are you? The commonsense approach says, "It's time to look inside and find out." But when you look up before looking in, you admit the need for an assessment that comes from outside of yourself. The Bible's assessment of our natural state is that we are *bent* in a particular direction. We are drawn toward independence, not dependence on God. Our selves naturally turn inward, like an ingrown toenail pointed in the wrong direction, causing discomfort.

This selfish impulse that turns us inward, away from God, is what the Bible calls sin. Earlier, we saw how sin manifests itself as a power, a condition, and in our personal choices. Now we need to see how sin affects the four D's.

Altered Design

First, sin leads us to resist or reject God's design for us. Like children who don't want to be told what to do by their parents, we want to choose our own path, to make our own way, to create our own reality. We want to be responsible for designing our lives, not conforming to a design that comes from outside ourselves.

The Bible says human beings are special because we are made in God's image and are designed to reflect his glory. But *we* say we are special because we have a glory all our own, a spark of uniqueness and creativity deep inside that needs to be unearthed and expressed. Sin alters our design by drawing us away from finding our role in a bigger story (that's not ultimately about us) and toward a manipulated view of the world where everyone else plays a part in our own story of self-fulfillment.

Altered Display

Sin changes the nature of our self-display as well. The Bible claims our ultimate purpose is to display the awesome creativity and power of God. Since sin turns us inward, our self-display becomes a means to receiving glory for ourselves. This hunger for self-focused glory shows up differently depending on the person. Some drop hints in conversation as to their own importance, while some shy away from the limelight but quietly manipulate others' perceptions.

In the internet age, everywhere we turn, people put themselves on display and invite feedback through comments and likes and other signals of affirmation. We can design the self we want others to see, display it, and then wait for a response in real time. Sin affects us by leading us to base our worth and value in the praise we receive from others.[23]

Not only that, the original purpose for which we were made is affected. Remember how we were designed to be a display, a reflection of God in different spheres of life? All of those spheres undergo an alteration. We were created to reflect God in how we relate to each other, but the selfish impulse infects our relationships and stirs up quarrels and resentment. When relationships break down at the personal level, the domino effect can lead to greater and greater conflict, until eventually entire nations go to war.

We were designed to reflect God in how we work, but because work often feels toilsome or unsatisfying, sin would have us either withdraw from work (through idleness or laziness) or search so much for satisfaction in our work that we can no longer conceive of ourselves apart from our job. In the former case, work becomes just a necessary evil. In the latter case, work becomes so necessary we define ourselves by it.

We were designed to reflect God in how we rest, but sin keeps our routines and rituals of rest from bringing fulfillment. Instead of experiencing rest as a deep and satisfying peace in the soul, we settle for mere entertainment, medicating ourselves by binging TV shows. Perpetually unfulfilled, chronically tired, we limp along in life while wondering how others seem so successful at chasing their dreams.

We were designed to exercise authority in whatever sphere of influence we've been given, but sin infects our ability to do so wisely. Some are tempted to abandon their rightful authority, refusing their responsibility, which leaves a void of leadership. Others are tempted to abuse their authority, wielding their position over people in order to demonstrate their power. In both cases, relationships suffer, people get hurt, and injustice spreads throughout society.

Sin is multifaceted in its ability to affect various spheres of life. Different people are drawn to different errors. We have different tendencies based on our backgrounds and personalities, but underneath these superficial distinctions we find the same general purpose (we were made to reflect God) and the same general flaw (sin). The specifics of how sin affects us will differ, but this selfish impulse is always present, eating away at our relationships, destroying our ability to find true and lasting joy, and filling us with anxiety rather than peace.

Deformed Desires

What happens to our desires? Sin deforms them. The world tells you to follow your heart no matter what, but as we saw earlier, your heart may lead you astray. The Bible warns against over-trusting your heart. Sometimes your heart leads you in the right direction; other times it's way off. Being led by the desires of your heart is good only if your desires are good—for you and for others.

The last thing parents should do is give their children everything they want. Why? Because kids aren't mature enough to know what they should want. They don't know what is good for them long-term. Immediate instincts and immature impulses dominate. That's why good parents work hard to form and shape the desires of their children so that they want the right things. It's childish to chase everything you want, which is why we define maturity by the ability to put your desires on the examination table in order to determine which are good and which are bad. We're told the way to happiness is to pursue your deepest desires, but unless we interrogate our desires, we're actually being told to act like children again—to go after short-term pleasures and succumb to selfish impulses.

Thankfully, some of the wiser self-help books encourage you to analyze your desires so you can make more informed choices based on which desires you believe are best to pursue. But the Bible goes a step further. When you look up rather than in, you find you are not the ultimate judge of what desires are right or wrong, good or bad. The Bible says we should put our desires on the table and then examine them in light of an external benchmark. You need a standard from outside yourself (up, not in) by which to judge the rightness or wrongness of whatever it is you want. Even more, the Bible claims the greater answer to the question of desire is not that you should always reject your heart or dismiss your desires, but that you need a *new* heart and *new* desires.

What we need most is to be changed into the kind of person who wants the right things. We'll see how that works a little later.

Self-Definition

Now we come to the last D: definition. How does sin affect the way we define ourselves? Once again, the selfish impulse shows up, causing us to pursue our own purpose and identity at the expense of others around us. We look in rather than up in order to define our lives, to define what "our truth" is.

The "look in" approach to life makes "be true to yourself" the greatest commandment. The second commandment follows closely: "affirm whatever self your neighbor chooses to be." The greatest sins, in this way of thinking, are to fail to be true to yourself by conforming to someone else's vision for your life, or to refuse to support someone else's personal life choices.

But when seen in light of the Bible, this "look in" approach to life appears to celebrate the self-centered, inward turn. It strengthens the selfish impulse. In contrast to this approach, the Bible says the greatest commandments are to love God with all your heart, soul, mind, and strength, and then your neighbor as yourself.[24]

Look up, and God is God; we were made to love and enjoy him. Look in, and you are God; the world exists to love and enjoy you.

The Solution to Sin

What's to be done? Everyone admits there are problems in the world, and most people recognize their personal failures and flaws. This is why we all, to some degree or another, feel guilty and ashamed.

So how do we respond to sin? In the "look in" view, if you're not satisfied with life, it's likely that you've not yet found your authentic self and asserted your independence. You are still conforming to something outside yourself. The Bible's take, however, is that sin keeps you from being satisfied. The problem is that you haven't conformed *enough* to God's purpose and design for your life. The "look in" view often says the feelings of guilt and unworthiness are the problem, and you need to uproot them from your heart. The "look up" view says the feelings of guilt and unworthiness are symptoms revealing a deeper disease—sin—and it's the selfish impulse that must be uprooted.

The "look in" solution to sin is reassertion—when you take charge of your heart and stand your ground on whatever path you've chosen for yourself. If someone questions you or calls you to turn around, you assume they don't have your best interests at heart because they are questioning your self-definition and your deepest desires. To compromise or conform would be to deny yourself, and this is perhaps the greatest threat to your personal happiness.

The "look up" solution to sin is something radically and refreshingly different than reassertion. It's repentance. It's the moment you doubt yourself instead of trust yourself, when you have your eyes opened to the wrong steps you've taken and the bad desires you've chased, when you recognize the ways in which your words and actions have hurt people around you. It's when your heart sinks at the thought, *I'm the problem*, but then rises at the realization, *I am not bound to this path I've been on. What if I turn around?* It's when you realize the solution to your biggest problems is not to look in, but to look up, because the source of your biggest problems is not in your own self-defined failures, but in the self-made mess created by your independence from the God who made you in the first place.

Repentance is what separates the "look in" from the "look up" approach. This is the key difference. But often you don't see the line of separation right away. For example, you may be a religious person who attends church regularly. You may think your approach to life is in line with the Bible, that you are a "look up" kind of person. Just remember this: going to church, reading your Bible, singing songs of praise—these activities can still be present in the life of someone whose approach is to look *in, around,* and then *up.* It's possible to busy yourself with countless religious activities yet still adopt the mind-set that makes religion just another way of affirming your own self-definition and deepest desires.

The moment you'll be able to tell if your approach to life is really to "look up" first is when you come into conflict because of some kind of personal sin. The moment you walk down a wrong path and someone else—a spouse, a friend, a colleague, a church member—challenges the choice you've made, that's when you'll know. Do you respond with reassertion (the "look in" solution) or repentance (the "look up" solution)?

When your faith community tells you it's not okay for you to leave your spouse and kids for another lover, or it's not okay to hoard resources and show off your wealth, or it's not okay to take a job that requires you to compromise ethically, or it's not okay to be indifferent to injustice that affects the neighbor you are called to love—how do you respond? It's in the cases when someone calls you out for going down a wrong path that you see your approach to life. If your response is to say, *No one else has any authority to speak into how I live my life!,* then no matter how much knowledge you have of the Bible or how many religious services you've attended, your priority is still to "look in" before you "look up." And in that approach to life, "looking up" is just a way to receive divine sanction or approval for the way of life you've chosen. Repentance or reassertion. That's the key difference.

All Affected

It doesn't matter, in the end, whether you are religious or not. Sin doesn't respect the boundaries of religious affiliation. If sin is a power, a condition, and a choice, if it is as truly pervasive and infectious as the Bible describes it, then religious activities can't hide the reality. We're all affected. The selfish impulse is common to all of us.

The idea that there are "good people" and "bad people"—that we all can mark ourselves on a graph of "better" or "worse" morally—is blown up by the Bible. When it comes to sin, the Bible is radically, scandalously egalitarian. We're all in the same boat. That includes me, too. You're not reading a book by an author who has everything figured out, and who is always pure of heart, true, and authentic. We're in this together, all affected and infected by sin that turns us inward instead of upward.

Even our best attempts at making things right—at getting outside ourselves, at reforming our desires, at changing how we are viewed, at masking the true state of our hearts, at redesigning and redefining ourselves again and again—are doomed to fail. Self-manufactured chemotherapy won't kill this cancer. Radiation won't rid you of it. The moment you feel you're making progress in one area, you find sin spreading to another.

The Bible paints a picture of our souls shriveling up and wasting away due to the disease of sin. Sin hollows us out until we're a mere shell of who we could be. Nothing destroys our ability to be gloriously authentic, to be the best version of ourselves, more than sin. What's more, the Bible looks forward down the long and lonely path of sin and tells us where it leads: death.

Sin leads to death, both physical and spiritual. It's the self-destruction of the soul. When you cut yourself off from God (who is the source of life), death always follows. It's as if God has planted you on this earth but you've decided to uproot yourself. No matter how much life you may have for a time, the withering process of death has begun. That's the lot of all humanity. This is our common plight. Our days are numbered. The grave awaits. Judgment follows.

The "look in" approach to life sees death and urges you to seize the moment, to be true to your heart, and to fulfill your purpose by finding happiness through contributing your unique gift to the world. The Bible, in one of its bleakest books of wisdom, shakes its head at that approach and offers a reflection from someone who lived that way, who did his best to capture and hold on to every bit of fleeting happiness possible, only to find all his attempts to be futile. Far from bringing joy, the glittery aspects of self-satisfaction and self-motivation just compounded the pain and emptiness of a life coming to an end.[25]

The challenge of the "look in" approach to life is that it can't stave off death. There are no internal resources you can draw from that will keep you from suffering and pain, no deep desires that will heal you of a terminal illness. Death defies our self-definitions. Death makes all our attempts at expressing ourselves look shallow and temporal. Death levels us all, just like sin does, and it forces us to come face to face with the superficial answers we often give to life's most profound questions: Who are you? What are you here for? What does it all mean? Death forces these questions upon us with greater intensity.

The "look up" approach described in the Bible provides an answer to the problem of death, just as it provides an answer to the problem of sin. But the answer is not an intellectual solution, a motivational speech, or a new list of religious exercises. It arrives in the story of a particular person, the most important person we read about in the Bible—Jesus of Nazareth. Next, we turn to this man's life and teaching, and we'll see what ancient wisdom he brings to rethinking the self.

Reflection Questions

How have you experienced the "selfish impulse" in your relationships with others?

What are some specific areas of your life where you find the selfish impulse is strongest?

When someone calls you out for something you've done wrong, is your natural reaction usually reassertion or repentance? Why?

CHAPTER 8

The Ancient Wisdom of Jesus

Before we turn our focus to Jesus of Nazareth and how his teaching informs the project of rethinking ourselves, we must make sure to avoid the easy, well-traveled path that would turn him into just another source of wisdom that adds a spiritual dimension to your life. Remember, in a world where common sense would have us look in before looking up, our natural way to approach the teaching of Jesus is to try to fit his wisdom into the life we've already defined for ourselves.

If you are going to truly rethink yourself, however, you have to get out of your world and into his. You have to set aside your own life story for a moment and enter into the story the Bible tells. Just as a great movie introduces you to its characters and draws you into its narrative, the Bible invites you into its story, too.

You may be skeptical about what the Bible says. Bits and pieces may be helpful or inspiring (a psalm or a proverb or a story), but you find much of it hard to read, much less believe: long lists of obscure and seemingly arbitrary laws, the thundering of the prophets, commands that seem outdated or irrelevant, and far-fetched stories of miraculous events. I understand your hesitancy. But I believe you'll find it worthwhile to jump into what a famous theologian described as "the strange new world within the Bible" so you can engage it on its own terms.

My purpose in this chapter is to summarize key aspects of the big story that the Bible tells so I can show how the whole narrative points to Jesus. Nothing can replace reading the Bible and the story of Jesus for yourself, of course, but I hope to provide a helpful overview of the bestselling book of all time.

The Story of the Bible

As we saw earlier, the Bible's story begins with a personal and powerful God. He created the world and everything in it, making human beings in his image to reflect his glory by knowing and loving him. We also saw how the presence of sin has infected everything in the world, skewing our sense of purpose and thwarting our attempts at living in wholeness and love. The world maintains traces of its original glory, but everywhere you look, you see the effects of evil and the presence of suffering. Beauty and tragedy, tranquility and disruption, wholeness and heartache—the world and all of us in it are like shattered mirrors, and none of us can escape the shards of glass uncut.

One of the foundational questions the Bible asks is, *How will God fix the problem of sin and suffering? The world has gone so wrong; is there any way he could make things right?*

The problem of sin is universal. The plan of God is particular. He calls one man—Abraham—and plucks him from among the people of the world in order to establish a special relationship with him. God promises to bless the whole world through Abraham's descendants.[26]

Abraham is stunned at this revelation, especially since he and his wife are elderly and don't have any children of their own. But all throughout the Bible, God keeps his promises, even when they seem impossible. (Abraham's story is only the first of many strange occurrences in the Bible where a birth comes about under unusual, supernatural circumstances.)

The story of the Bible follows the trek of Abraham and his family, generation after generation. His grandson Jacob is given a new name "Israel,"[27] and from this point on, much of the Bible follows the journey of the "children of Israel." After a four-hundred-year sojourn in Egypt, during which the children of Israel are oppressed and enslaved, God intervenes, revealing his power through a series of plagues meant to embarrass the ruler of Egypt and his empire. God rescues his people through the faithfulness and leadership of a man named Moses.

After he has executed his rescue plan and led the people on the way toward a land he promised them, God makes clear his special relationship with Israel. The people were to be a *display* (there's that word again) of his glory, a light to the nations that would show the world what it looks like when God reigns as king and human beings live according to his design. God gave the people the Ten Commandments and numerous other laws to guide them in their personal and common life.[28] As the centuries unfolded, this group of former slaves made their way into the land God had promised them, where they established a kingdom and were ruled by men like David (who wrote the famous Psalm 23) and Solomon (whose perspective on life is found in the Bible's books of wisdom).

Let's recap the story so far. Human beings were designed to be a display of God's goodness and love. But this design has been altered because of sin, and the purpose of humanity in reflecting God has been derailed. To make things right, God chose and formed a people who were called to once again display his goodness and love. Unfortunately, the children of Israel were infected with the same disease as everyone else in the world. Sin is no respecter of persons (or peoples).

Whenever Israel went astray, God would raise up prophets to call his people to turn around, to abandon the wrong path, and to reengage and embrace again the God who had led them out of Egypt.[29] In the "look up" approach to life, the proper response to sin is repentance—turning away from sin and looking up again to God. And over the centuries, the Bible offers glimmers of hope, where Israel leaned more fully into her calling to be a special people, set apart as a light to the world. But more often, the Bible records disappointment and failure. The presence of sin not only separates us from God; it separates us from other people, and this division became evident when Israel split into two different kingdoms. The northern kingdom was conquered by armies that scattered and dispersed the people. The people of the southern kingdom were taken into exile and had to learn how to be God's people while in a foreign land.

Disillusioned and disoriented, the children of Israel cried out to God, pleading with him to keep his promise to establish them once again in the land he had promised, under his rule alone. Decades later, some of the people were given permission to return to their homeland and rebuild the temple and the city walls around the capital city of Jerusalem.[30] But it was never the same. The land was occupied and controlled by foreign armies, and the people still experienced oppression and injustice.

Into this world of anticipation and anxiety, where people were waiting for God to raise up a king who would turn things around and make everything right, comes Jesus of Nazareth.

The reason I've offered this brief overview of biblical history is so that you'll see Jesus not as merely a great teacher, or a spiritual guru, or a divine butler who exists to serve you and make your life better. If we are to engage the Bible as it really is, and see Jesus as he is presented, we must understand the history surrounding his story. To pull him from his context creates the risk of making him nothing more than an avenue toward a more spiritually fulfilling life as we conceive it.

Jesus the Teacher

Yet, even though Jesus is *more* than a teacher, he is a teacher. And as we look at his life, we can start with this aspect. Even if you are unconvinced that Jesus was born of a virgin, or that he is the Son of God or the Savior of the world, you likely maintain a level of respect for his teaching. You may question the faithfulness of his followers or whether he deserves the exalted titles that Christians give him, but you cannot deny his role as a teacher whose words have had a major impact on the world. Even in the "look in" approach to life, the commonsense take on Jesus is that he's the kind of teacher who is going to have *something* valuable to offer you.

But what exactly did he teach? When we look at the Bible's record of Jesus' teachings, we encounter someone who doesn't fit the mythical image so often presented to us, both in the church and in wider society. If you grew up going to church, you may think of Jesus as a barely human figure, a spiritual superman whose main work was to assure a heavenly afterlife for his followers. If you've gotten your information about Jesus from American culture, you may think of him as the ultimate cheerleader for the "look in" approach to life—a nonjudgmental, harmless teacher whose role is to give his spiritual blessing to you as you define yourself, chase your dreams, and seek affirmation of your uniqueness.

The problem is that the Gospels—the four biographies of Jesus we find in the Bible—paint a very different picture. Jesus' teaching fits neither the image popular among many churchgoers nor the "look in" approach popular in our society.

Jesus Pointing Up

First, Jesus—like the rest of the Bible—starts with God and not with us. He's the best example of anyone in history who starts with the "look up" approach to life. The central message of his teaching is this: "The time is fulfilled, and the kingdom of God has come near. Repent and believe the good news!"[31]

The kingdom of God refers to the rule of God, or the reign of God. When Jesus made this announcement, he meant that God was returning to Israel to set up his rule once again. In other words, *Get ready! Everyone's about to see what it looks like when God shows up as king.*

What's the proper response to this message? Faith and repentance. Faith is when you believe in the good news that God is making good on his promise to fix everything. Repentance is getting ready for the future by turning around from a self-focused life and turning instead to God.

Take a look at society today and you'll see different groups offering different solutions for how to make things right in the world. *Everything's a mess! Here's how we fix it.* The same was true in Jesus' time. Some of his contemporaries were revolutionaries, others were compromisers, while still others wanted to withdraw from society altogether. Different groups had different agendas, but they all expected God to come alongside and bless their plans. Jesus' way stood out. He rejected all the various plans on offer and said the people should follow his path instead—a controversial way of life that would abandon any aim of revolution and cultivate instead a heartfelt love for enemies and a deep sense of trust in God's plan to remake the world.

With that in mind, if we were to travel back in time and join the original listeners of Jesus' message, we'd realize that "to repent" means we must abandon whatever path we were going down. We wouldn't have all the negative associations we have with that word in our culture; we would know it is simply a call to trade in our own ideas of what would make our lives better and choose instead to follow the kingdom agenda as laid out by Jesus. It also means we would have to reject and renounce sin—the destructive power that defaces the good world God has made, as well as the condition that infects us all with the selfish impulse.

We could put it this way: for Jesus, to repent means you move from looking *in* as the starting point of your life to looking *up*. You reject the selfish impulse to make God a bit player in your personal agenda. You don't bring God into your dream for your life; instead you bring yourself in line with God's dream for the world. He's not part of your personal kingdom or success story;

you accept his kingdom agenda and rethink success by his definition of faithfulness.

Jesus Turning Upside Down

The path Jesus proposed was fundamentally at odds with the way many of the people of his day saw the world. He kicked off his most famous sermon by turning upside down commonsense wisdom about human happiness and flourishing. In a world where successful people were wealthy and proud, full of laughter and food and plans to lord their authority over others, Jesus offered a different vision. The people flourishing according to God's good design for the world were those most likely to look up, those whose spirits were downcast and impoverished, leading them to recognize how little they had without God. God's blessing fell not on the self-driven and self-satisfied, but on those who wept over the state of the world and mourned the state of their own hearts. The people flourishing according to God's design were those who hungered not for riches and glory but for justice and goodness, who showed mercy, who were known for gentleness and kindness, who stepped into conflicts and took fire from both sides because they extended their arms to make peace.[32]

The reason Jesus' teaching resonated with people in his day and still resonates in ours is that his words still surprise us in how they turn upside down our common-sense expectations about what we need in order to live well. His teaching was revolutionary then, and it's revolutionary now—to the point we often try to soften or explain away the harder aspects of his teaching.

Jesus' way counters the "look in" approach to life head-on. As we've seen, surveys show more than 90 percent of Americans claiming that to find yourself, you must look inside yourself.

Jesus says the way to find your self is to lose it, and when you lose your self, that's how you'll find it.[33]

Jesus asks what good it is if you gain everything you want in the world and yet lose your soul.[34]

When he does speak of looking within ourselves, Jesus tells us that evil is not just something that happens *to* us, but is something that bubbles up from *inside* us.[35] All our words—including the hurtful and untruthful ones—are the overflow of our hearts. From our hearts come our actions.[36]

When you look closely at the teachings of Jesus, you don't get the sense that the purpose of life is to go off on your own, look into your heart, discover who you want to be, and then emerge triumphantly with a self that deserves affirmation. Instead, you come into contact with a man filled with unmovable conviction and unmistakable compassion. He calls and commands. He lays out a way of life and presses for a life-altering decision to follow him. He makes demands on us, calls us to give up certain things, and in all this gives the impression that obeying his call will free us, not shackle us.[37]

But in case you think Jesus has his sights set only on the "look in" approach to life, you shouldn't miss the ways in which Jesus challenges the "look around" approach to life also. In cultures where the opinion of your family or community matters more than anything else—where looking around takes priority over looking up—Jesus' words land with terrible force. He forms a new family around himself and claims that allegiance to his upside-down kingdom takes precedent over anyone else you might "look around" to in order to discover who you are and your purpose in life. Mother, father, sister, brother—Jesus says you must hate them all if you are to follow him.[38] A shocking bit of hyperbole, yes, but Jesus wanted to make his point clear. You look *up* first, not in, and not around.

Everything and everyone else who could claim your ultimate allegiance—including your family, your religious tradition, your country, and yes, even your own self—must fall away in terms of priority. There can be no misunderstanding. To follow Jesus doesn't mean you add him to your "look around" approach to life, or make him part of your personal journey of looking inside yourself.

Jesus calls for a total reorientation of the heart by saying, *Start with me alone.*

We've been conditioned to think that learning to love yourself is an important first step on the road to emotional health and happiness. And, of course, a healthy evaluation of our worth and value as people made in the image of God is important and necessary for us to flourish. But more often than not, self-love in Scripture is not a path to freedom and happiness, but a cul-de-sac that leads us around in circles of frustration. Self-love easily succumbs to the selfish impulse that is the mark of sin.

For this reason, Jesus tells us that we must walk the way of self-sacrifice, a road marked by dying daily to our old self as we are transformed as his followers.[39] Jesus sweeps away all our preconceived notions about high self-esteem leading to happiness and claims instead that true life requires dying to our selfish impulses. Finding yourself requires dying to yourself and to all the desires that are bad for you and bad for the world. Following Jesus means dying to the approach in which you are the maker of meaning, the definer of your life. As one Bible teacher has put it:

> The self we are to deny, disown, and crucify is our fallen self, everything within us that is incompatible with Jesus Christ.

> The self we are to affirm and value is our
> created self, everything within us that is
> compatible with Jesus Christ. True self-
> denial is not the road to self-destruction,
> but the road to self-discovery.[40]

What's more, Jesus blasts the whole notion of displaying our selves and our goodness for others to see and approve. The notion of doing good or being good as a way of signaling to others how virtuous and holy we are wilts under the unrelenting light of God's utter perfection. Jesus condemns the desire to be seen as respectable, to do good things in order to be seen by others and affirmed.[41] He is not impressed when your attempts at being a good person are really just efforts to be *seen* as a good person.

To be clear, Jesus is not opposed to doing good things, but he makes a contrast between the good and bad motivations behind our self-display. The good way of displaying yourself is when your acts of love and mercy and justice reflect the character of God, so that when people see your goodness, they praise *him*.[42] The bad way of displaying yourself is when your acts of love and mercy and justice are just another way of fulfilling the selfish impulse, so that people see you doing good and praise *you*.[43]

As kids we sing, "This little light of mine, I'm going to let it shine." The "look in" interpretation of that song means you're shining your light so that others will see your specialness and uniqueness. The "look up" interpretation means you're letting your light shine so that more and more people will praise God.

Hard to Hear

If you read the Gospels, you'll find yourself nodding along at some of Jesus' sayings and stories. You will admire his love for the outcast, his emphasis on generosity, and his teaching that we are to show kindness and forgiveness to people no matter their cultural background. Many of Jesus' most famous stories (the Prodigal Son, the Good Samaritan, the Lost Sheep) have become so well-known that they have been incorporated into what passes for common sense in the world.

You will also read about how Jesus was known for miracles that seemed to bring back a little bit of God's original design to a world thrown into chaos because of sin—whether it was stopping a windstorm with a word, or giving sight to a man born blind, or healing people with various ailments, or freeing people oppressed by dark spiritual forces.[44] Everywhere he went, light appeared and invaded the darkness.

But some aspects of Jesus' teaching often get neglected. They don't fit neatly in the "Inspiration" section of a bookstore. And one of the biggest stumbling blocks for people reading Jesus for the first time is when you hear what he says about himself. The exalted language that Christians use when speaking of Jesus didn't show up out of nowhere. Jesus spoke in ways that implied that he saw himself on par with God.[45] He did things that God alone was supposed to do, like pronounce someone's sins forgiven.[46] Jesus not only demonstrated through his actions the kind of person he was; he also spoke about himself in ways that seemed borderline blasphemous.[47]

Another stumbling block is the paradox of Jesus' radical inclusivity and exclusivity. He was called the "friend of sinners"[48] because he welcomed all kinds of people, no matter their sins and struggles, to the table of repentance, even if the religious leaders would have written them off due to the nature of their sins. His inclusive embrace was scandalous, and it angered the religious elite.[49] At the same time, Jesus was radically exclusive, claiming that he alone was the way, and that no one gets to God except through him.[50] He described his path as narrow, not broad, and claimed there is only one gate to God, not many.[51] And when he laid out his moral vision for the world, he refused to relax or lessen the older laws in the Bible, choosing instead to intensify them based on God's original design.[52]

When Jesus spoke about the kingdom of God—the rule and reign of God breaking into the world, he meant his message to bring both comfort and warning. We like the comfortable side of that message, especially in an era when "looking up" is merely the path toward inspiration. But if we are to truly hear Jesus on his own terms, we must not ignore the disturbing part of his message.

Is it comforting to hear that God will make everything right again? Yes. Is it a warning to hear that God will make everything right again? Yes. Why a warning? Because if God is going to make everything right, he is going to do away with everything wrong. You don't distinguish what is right and what is wrong unless you exercise judgment. And that means, unless you're part of what is right in the world, you're going to be on the wrong side of his justice whenever God judges the world.

God the Judge

As soon as we begin talking about God's judgment, your mind may race to a view of God as a distant, impersonal authority figure who holds the world to the letter of the law and gleefully looks for reasons to condemn people for the slightest infraction. Such is the caricature of judgment as many people understand Christianity today. The church is all about judgment, and the world is all about acceptance, or so goes the commonsense take on religion in society. But this simplistic view of judgment doesn't do justice to the Bible's actual teaching, and it also fails to note how our society may be more awash in judgment than ever.

In recent years, I've been intrigued by the number of people on New Year's Eve who wish others a "judgment-free" year. Isn't it interesting that the best wishes we muster up on the night before the calendar changes fall in line with the "look in" approach to life? *Here's to a year of being what you want to be and doing what you want to do, no matter what other people may say or how you might be judged!* Why does a culture that prioritizes "looking in" still long to escape judgment? Doesn't this wish for a judgment-free year indicate that many of us feel judged and guilty all the time? Whether it's the inner critic we can't silence, or the raised eyebrow from people around us, we feel that judgment is still ever present.

The rise of social media has thrown a spotlight on our judgmentalism. If you say something inappropriate, or take a stance that others disagree with, or if you post a picture or make a statement that others do not approve of, you'll find out just how judgmental our society is. Research shows that more young people today suffer from mental health problems, and the spike in mental illness is linked to time spent on the smartphone, often in social environments that create a fear of judgment and desire for affirmation.[53] The fear of getting "canceled" makes many people constantly feel guilt-ridden and anxious.

How would the "look in" approach have us respond to these feelings of guilt and judgment that we can't seem to shake? Common sense says you should look inside yourself and make yourself the judge of your life. You determine for yourself the standard you want to live up to. You determine right and wrong for yourself. Feelings of guilt are illegitimate, and the way to avoid them is to "shut out the noise" from the rest of the world and to dismiss what anyone else thinks about your life. Your life is a test, and you are the grader. No one else. You determine what success and failure look like for you, and then you judge yourself.

The "look up" approach is radically different. You don't avoid the feelings of guilt, but press deeper into them, looking for the root cause. While some guilt may be illegitimate and the result of blaming ourselves for things that are not our fault, the Bible teaches that many feelings of guilt point to the diagnosis of sin. And the right response is not to look inside yourself and set your own standard, but to look up and measure yourself by an outside standard—something that transcends both what you'd define for yourself, and what looking around to others might define for you. Looking up puts your self-judgment, or the judgment you sense from others, in a different perspective. *God is your judge.*

That's both good news and bad news. It sounds like bad news at first, because, truth be told, we say we don't want to be judged at all, especially if it involves failing to measure up to a higher standard set for us by God. But the good news is, in a world awash in condemnation, where people make judgments and hurl insults all the time, where we find it hard to silence the inner critic that tells us we are without worth and value, there's freedom in looking past your self and your community to say: *God is the one who judges me.*

That's not to say it doesn't matter what other people think of you or what you think of yourself, only that what God says about you matters more. God's judgment relativizes all human judgments, including your own. There's no escape from judgment. If you never judge yourself, you'll wither under the judgments of others around you. If you withdraw from the judgments of others around you, you'll be a rough judge on yourself, always wondering if you're truly being the best you can be, wondering what faults you have that you can't see, and feeling insecure because you don't have any outside standard of goodness or success. The only solution is to look *up* and say, *God is my judge.*

According to the Bible, God is the one judge who is always consistent. The ancient songs in the middle of the Bible—the psalms—rejoice in the idea of God as judge because God's judgment means that the Maker of this earth is going to make things right again.[54] All that's wrong with the world will be done away with. And so we're back to the comfort and the warning of this message. The comfort is that God is going to fix everything. The warning is that you're part of what needs to be fixed.

People looking for inspiration love the comfort but not the warning. Judgmental people love the warning, but not the comfort. But Jesus holds both out to us, and to truly hear him on his own terms, we must come to a point of decision. Like the people who first followed him, we must consider a number of questions. *Is this man who he says he is? Can he do what he says he will do? Is his way best for me and for the world?* These questions raise additional ones: *If God is my judge, what does that mean for me? I've got issues. I've got sins. I've got problems. I've hurt people. Jesus says that he forgives sins. Can he forgive mine? If so, how? Is there a way for God to execute justice as a judge and also show mercy to people who mess up?*

The good news we find in the Bible is that God isn't just interested in helping us; he's committed to rescuing us. And it's not in what Jesus *said* that we find the ultimate way of rethinking ourselves, but in what Jesus *did*. That's what makes looking *up* even possible.

The event at the heart of the Bible and at the heart of the Christian faith is the hinge of history and the explosive source of all life transformation.[55] That's what we must look at next.

Reflection Questions

What parts of Jesus' life and teaching are most familiar to you? What parts of his teaching are surprising or hard to swallow?

What would it look like if everyone lived according to Jesus' "look up" approach? How would your life change?

How do you respond to the idea of "self-denial" for the sake of greater happiness? How do self-denial and self-discovery work together?

CHAPTER 9

The Hinge of History

Because we've been conditioned to the "look in" approach to life, we expect the answer to rethinking ourselves will show up in a package of principles, a new code of conduct, or a book full of inspirational advice. But the Bible turns our expectations upside down, offering not advice but an announcement. Not an explanation of how to change your life but a series of events that have changed the world. We're expecting an infomercial and instead get a news flash.

In order to understand the heart of this news flash, we must take a closer look at a central aspect of the story line of the Bible: the elaborate sacrificial system central to the life of Israel.

Over the centuries, as the children of Israel—the people through whom God promised to make things right—made their way in the world, there was the lingering question of how to deal with their own sin. Whether we are talking about sin as a power, a condition, or an action, there's one thing it always does: it spreads. Though they tried to be a light to the nations, the selfish impulse had spread among everyone, including the people of God. This selfishness was responsible for breaking their relationship with God again and again, as well as breaking the relationship between people.

The sacrificial system, with its detailed lists of rules and regulations, functioned like a quarantine intended to keep the spread of sin's presence and power from overtaking the community. It also provided a way for someone personally to be absolved of guilt and shame. There were different sacrifices for different situations, but the heart of the sacrificial system was the idea that someone's sin and guilt was transferred to the animal being slaughtered in his or her place.[56] Something had to be done with the darkness of sin swirling around and in the people of God, and the sacrificial system provided a way for a person to be set right with God and reconciled to other people.

The Sacrificial Scapegoat

As gruesome or primitive or superstitious as sacrifice may sound, you shouldn't overlook the ways in which "modern" societies—including ours—still act according to a similar logic. Take the description of someone as the "scapegoat." Injustice and corruption are revealed in an organization, and before long, everyone is pointing fingers every which way, trying to keep the blame from falling on their shoulders. If enough people begin pointing fingers in the same direction, and if outside observers who are outraged by the corruption they've witnessed begin to agree on where the blame should fall, usually one leader—whether or not they were personally at fault or just minimally involved—will wind up losing their job and reputation. Once that happens, the organization resets. All the pent-up fury over corruption falls on one person, and then everything restarts, though hopefully not without some soul searching and a new determination to avoid the same problems in the future. Someone "took the fall" so the rest of the organization could survive.

We see the same phenomenon in online outrage. A prominent person's problematic words or actions from the past come to light. Accusations multiply—some true, some false—and then criticism builds, with more and more people joining the chorus, until the situation reaches a breaking point. The person might apologize for their previous words or actions, but depending on the severity of the infraction, the chorus of critics could get louder and louder until the person sees no other way forward but to resign their position, lose their status, or be chased out of public life.

The scapegoat mentality may seem ancient and outdated, especially in a "look in" world where everyone is supposed to be free to say or do what they want (as long as they don't interfere with everyone else saying and doing what they want). But what if we are not as free from judgment as we think we are? What if we only think we are in control of our lives and our path forward in the world, but are actually more influenced by others than we care to admit? What if the supposedly primitive way of dealing with sin and its effects is still with us today, although the manifestation is different?

The presence of a sacrificial system reinforces a central truth: sin has consequences. Someone must "take the fall." Someone must pay the debt. We prefer the illusion that we are free to chase our dreams and pursue whatever we desire the most, but the selfish impulse that infects those dreams and desires always leads to unintended consequences.

What if following your heart when you're married means you pursue a person you're attracted to, even if that course of action would devastate your spouse and break up your family? You may have some friends who'd say, "Go for it! You deserve to be happy. Why should you sacrifice your happiness for the sake of your family?" But other friends may say, "This is the wrong path. You've got to resist the bad desire because you'll ruin the lives of people you love, and the happiness you think you'll achieve would come at too great a cost. You're sacrificing your family." In a world where you look inside yourself and then around for support, which set of friends would you be more likely to listen to? Furthermore, if looking up comes last and you do consider how God would see your situation, you may think to yourself, *God wants me to be happy, doesn't he? God wouldn't give me desires that he didn't want me to fulfill.* And since God approves of your pursuit of happiness, even if he doesn't approve of all your choices, he'll still forgive you in the end because, well, we all make mistakes, and it's God's job to forgive, right?

Now imagine a world in which this way of thinking isn't limited to you but becomes common sense for everybody. The selfish impulse infects our process of looking in to find happiness, and our pursuit of desires leads to consequences that would sacrifice the happiness of others. Sin and sacrifice always go together. Sin in the community (often revealed through injustice, oppression, and corruption) spreads whenever people pursue desires that result in harm toward others. Then, in response to corruption, many people react in ways that, because of the selfish impulse in perpetrators and victims alike, further the chain reaction. One group pursues its well-being at the expense of another group, until retaliation and revenge become normal and the cycle of vengeance—seen in skirmishes, battles, and wars—threatens to tear apart the fabric of society. When cultures descend into the darkness of such selfishness, people sometimes wonder out loud if some kind of demonic force or dark spiritual presence has invaded the world. Sinful actions that stem from our sinful condition lead to speculation about Sin as a power with a mind all its own.

The sacrificial system described in the Bible was an ancient way of "resetting" things personally and societally, in order to build a barrier against the waves of brokenness unleashed by the tsunami of sin and selfishness. The rituals provided a picture of the reality of sin, and through the offering of a sacrificial lamb or the sending away of a scapegoat, they provided a way of reconciliation and restoration in one's relationship with God and with others.

The more "modern" we feel, the more we may sneer at this notion, but in a world plagued by vengeance and feelings of guilt, we'd be better off asking why sacrifices have been so prevalent throughout world history and why we continue to act in ways that give credence to these ancient patterns of thought. The feeling of helplessness before Sin as a power, the guilt and shame over our sinful condition and actions, and the desire to see something accomplished that would bring resolution by ridding us of the weight of all this pain and paying the price for our selfishness—this feeling cries out within us, *Won't someone, somewhere fix all this?*

The Death of Jesus

Here is where Jesus steps in, not just as someone who taught us the way of wisdom, but as *someone who died.* For several reasons, including the scandalous inclusivity of his welcome and the exclusivity of his self-perception, as well as his refusal to get on board with any of the agendas of his people who hoped to see revolutionary action against the Roman Empire, Jesus became a threat both to the religious establishment and political authorities. The conspiracy against him led to the charge that he had set himself up as a king who opposed the Roman government.

Was Jesus really guilty of sedition against the Romans? No. When asked a trick question about taxes, Jesus said, "Give to Caesar the things that are Caesar's, and to God the things that are God's"[57]—another way of saying that in terms of priority, we look up before we look around. Jesus' cryptic statement didn't deny our obligations to other people or the country to which we belong. But it did relativize our earthly responsibilities by calling us to give God what rightly belongs to him—our whole lives. God first—not government, not your family, and not even yourself.

Jesus told his people to love their enemies, to go the extra mile if a Roman soldier commanded it, and to turn the other cheek.[58] Jesus was innocent of the charge of sedition. He never called for revolution against Rome. But through the conspiring of corrupt men among the people of God (Israel) and the foreign rulers (Rome), Jesus was delivered up to be executed by crucifixion. He became the ultimate scapegoat.

As his popularity plummeted, the hands that once waved him into the city as the fulfiller of their own desires and dreams for the world now pointed their fingers at him. The chants of the people grew louder, and the cries of "Crucify him!" swelled into a sadistic screech of vengeance until, at long last, the deed was done. Jesus was stripped of his dignity, tortured to the brink of death, and pinned to a cross like an insect where he slowly suffocated in his own blood.[59]

The Difference in This Death

Looking at this execution in historical context, we may be inclined to shake our heads at just another example in a long line of injustices perpetrated by the Roman government, another crucifixion designed to remind everyone who was in charge. Crucifixions were not uncommon in the first century. This cruel and shameful manner of death made a display of the criminal in order to quash any seditious or revolutionary desires in the hearts of the people.

But there was something different about the death of Jesus: he had predicted it. He had said that he would go to the cross.[60] When you read the historical accounts of his life, it's as if all the miracles he performed and the stories he told were merely the prelude to his most important act—dying.

What's more, Jesus and his future biographers quoted regularly from the ancient Scriptures when talking about his death. They didn't see this moment as an unfortunate circumstance for the wrong man in the wrong place at the wrong time; they believed that somehow, in some way, this execution was part of a greater plan. They believed the Creator who designed the world and saw the spread of sin's infection had a master plan to fix everything—a plan that involved the sacrifice of an innocent man.

Not only that, even when Jesus shrank back from the fate that awaited him, we still see in his words and actions the willing embrace of this role of scapegoat and sacrifice.[61] He did not turn away from the valley of the shadow of death but willingly walked into the darkness. It seems he knew that, in some mysterious way, his death was the showdown between good and evil, between the power of God and the forces of darkness that plague our world. Although crucifixions were meant to display the selfish power of Rome, *this* crucifixion displayed the self-giving love of God. For in that moment, even as he died, Jesus breathed out words of forgiveness and faith, taking upon himself the sins of the world and suffering under the full consequences of those sins, just like a sacrifice. Even though he was innocent, Jesus "took the fall."

Of course, what stands out most about the death of Jesus is that his followers claimed to have seen him alive again a few days later. And for a period of forty days, Jesus continued to appear to people, leading up to a moment when his followers saw him disappear, and they concluded that this was no ordinary earthly king, but the exalted king of the world.

Here we come to the extraordinary claim at the heart of the Bible's teaching about Jesus: the man who willingly went to the cross and died in our place got up and walked out of his grave, and is now King over the universe, worthy of allegiance from everyone on earth.

If you think that sounds unbelievable, you're not alone. It sounded crazy back then, too. (Ancient people didn't need a modern scientist to inform them that dead people stay dead.) You may not have a good explanation of what happened to his early followers, or how the body disappeared from the tomb, or why these rumors took hold of so many people so quickly. It's understandable if you think the story sounds farfetched or strange. I like how Sarah Ruden, a translator of ancient classics, puts it:

> [Christianity] arose when a small group of Jews became convinced that their leader, a poor and relatively uneducated man from the tiny town of Nazareth (a backwater of the backwater Galilee), whom the Romans had tortured to death as a troublemaker, had risen from the dead and ascended into heaven, thus delivering mankind from sin and death—and that this was the point of all existence in the universe. As unscientific as it makes us seem, I and two billion-plus other people say, "of course."[62]

My point here is not to compile all the reasons why you should believe this news is true. (You can find other books that examine and investigate the evidence.[63]) My goal is to help you see how the Bible itself tells the story of the world and the story of Jesus. If you're going to rethink yourself and give full consideration to the "look up" approach to life, it's important to inhabit the world of the Bible for a little longer.

In the biblical narrative, we see how those who knew Jesus and saw him after his death became convinced that something extraordinary had happened. They believed this man had become the ultimate scapegoat and sacrifice who had willingly accepted the blame and absorbed the cost of all the sin in the world.[64] They believed this man had received the judgment he had warned about, and that something of a *reset* had taken place. The meaning of the cross was redemptive: sin had been taken care of, the forces of evil had been defeated, and the selfish impulse of humanity had been overcome by a flood of self-giving love. No more sacrifices were needed; this was the final, universal sacrifice for sin.

The resurrection made Jesus' followers go back to their ancient Scriptures and reread everything in light of this extraordinary event, and when they did, they came to the conclusion that Jesus wasn't just an ordinary man, or even an exceptional man, but that in some mysterious way, he was the embodiment of God himself. He was both the ultimate display of what God always intended a human being to be (fulfilling God's original design) and also the ultimate expression of God's desire for the world.

Slowly but surely, over the course of the following years and decades, the earliest Christians began to rethink everything, seeing Jesus as the image of God, the display of his glory and character. As they contemplated the cross and resurrection of Jesus, they began to rethink what it means to desire God above all else, and what it means when the desire of God is to be known and loved by his people, because only in knowing and loving him do we find our greatest joy. Design, display, desire . . . and then they worked backwards to a new definition of who Jesus must be—God in human form, God among us, fully God and fully man at the same time.

Rethinking the World

There's a lot of *rethinking* going on in the Bible, and most of it comes from rethinking the world in light of the cross and resurrection of Jesus. The later writers of the Bible saw this as the pivotal moment in world history. This is what makes sense of the whole story of the whole world. This is what fulfills all the ancient prophecies. This is the event that changes everything.

If you want to take the final step in understanding the "look up" approach to life, you need to consider the earliest followers of Jesus as they sorted out their lives in light of these extraordinary events. In letters from early Christian leaders to the early churches, we find a lot about life transformation and the difference between a person's "old self" and "new self."

The latter parts of the Bible tell us what personal renewal looks like in light of what Jesus did. It's about looking up, around, and then in. It's about having your mind and heart changed—with your desires shifting and your display changed and a fully redesigned person emerging. Even if you still have doubts about the meaning of the cross or the reality of the resurrection, it's worth giving the Bible a chance to speak into the project of rethinking yourself. The death and resurrection of Jesus changes the way we view the four D's and makes true transformation possible.

Reflection Questions

When have you seen someone you love "pay the price" for someone else's selfishness? When have you been hurt by others living selfishly?

How does the death of Jesus on the cross resolve the problem of sin and selfishness, according to the Bible?

How do you view the resurrection of Jesus? How would believing Jesus was raised from the dead change the way you live?

CHAPTER 10

Your New Self

There are two dangers that threaten any attempt at rethinking yourself in light of the Bible. The first danger is that you interpret any talk about a "new self" or a "new path" as just another religious lifestyle that involves a new set of rules. Religion equals rules. In other words, you move away from the good *news* about Jesus to good *advice* about how to live a decent, moral life.

This danger is ever present because, for many in our society, *being religious is all about being a good person.* Morality is the point of religion. What you believe doesn't matter as much as how you behave. This is why there are some who attend religious services, or send their kids to camp, or encourage their teenagers' involvement in church activities, not because they believe in the good news that changes everything, but because religion helps cultivate a sense of decency and morality among people.

Within this environment, it's easy to hear talk about obedience, or living in a way that is set apart from others, or being more like Jesus, and revert to a morality-centered or rules-based approach to rethinking yourself. The problem is that this mentality takes us back to the "look in" approach to life. It's all about you and your personal improvement. Once again we've turned inward first, and used religion to fuel our self-fulfillment project.

The second danger is one I mentioned earlier: you turn the good news of Jesus into something merely inspirational. Religion equals inspiration. You turn to your faith for solace when you need comfort or when you confront a challenge. This danger takes us back to the "look in" approach as well, because it puts us at the center of our story and turns Jesus into a spiritual guide who just helps us get through the day.

These two dangers are prevalent in a society that believes all religions are basically the same and that the purpose of religion is to help you become a moral and decent person or to help you make sense of your life and find some purpose. So, whether you encounter the temptation to make faith all about morals or all about inspiration, the end result is the same: you're looking in before looking up. And looking up is what the Bible insists again and again we prioritize.

Letters Looking Up

One thing stands out when you read the letters written by the first followers of Jesus: they usually start by pointing *up*. They direct our attention upward.

The apostle Paul is the writer of more letters in the Bible than anyone else, and in his writings we find an early leader's instructions to small congregations of followers of Jesus about how to read the story of the world in light of Jesus' death and resurrection. Like the other writers, Paul usually began by pointing *up*.

In his most famous letter, written to Roman Christians, Paul starts out by summing up the announcement of Jesus the King who has fulfilled all of God's ancient promises to his people.[65] In his letter to the Ephesians, Paul devotes attention to God's ultimate plan to put the world back together—a cosmic unveiling of how God will make all things new, with Jesus at the center of the plan, and his followers being rescued from death and put in right relationship with him.[66] Paul's letter to the Galatians stands out because he jumps right to his main concern: the followers of Jesus in this community are abandoning the truth for lies.[67] But even here, Paul is pointing his readers upward, away from the idea that it's their own goodness that serves as the basis for being rescued by God, and reminding them of God's grace. Paul insists that they've been put in right relationship with God and belong to his people not because they've performed all the religious rites and deserve salvation, but solely due to the mercy and grace of God.

Living in light of the cross and resurrection, according to the earliest followers of Jesus, means that we start by looking *up* to who God is and what he has done, and then *around* to the new community that we have been given, and finally *in* at what God is doing in us, through us, and for us. This is the "look up" approach to life, and it's what we see in the Bible. And, of course, it's the reverse of how so many in our society see their life's meaning and purpose. Let's consider the four D's again, but this time in light of the Bible's "look up" approach.

A New Design

Looking up starts not with definition, but design. The starting point for following Jesus is when you get the redesign you've always longed for but could never pull off.

Remember when we discussed how people—anxious and fretting about their lives on display for others—often feel the need to adopt a new persona, or put on a new face and become a different person? Whether the redesign is physical (workouts, diets, makeovers), vocational (a new job or career), or educational (going back to school or picking up a new hobby), the point is that we often become dissatisfied with our lives, and so we long for a redesign. Social media provides a shortcut, giving us the chance to change our online persona faster than we can change our bodies or our hearts. We may start displaying something new to the world even before it reflects the truth about us.

In a nighttime conversation with a religious leader, Jesus described the ultimate redesign as being "born again." (The term could also be translated "born from above."[68] Once again, the point is to look *up*!) Other words we could use to describe this redesign are "conversion" or "transformation" or "life change."

The difference with the Bible's redesign is that it goes beyond the superficial elements we might associate with a spiritual makeover (being religious, adopting spiritual activities); it is a supernatural event, something that can't be fully explained by old ways of thinking. It is so drastic that it can be compared to a new birth—which also means that it isn't something you do for God; it's something God does for you.

What does this look like practically? How does someone undergo this new birth? For many people, the experience comes about when—after becoming familiar with Jesus and having seen the transformation that happens to people who orient their lives around him—they feel an inner stirring of conviction that includes sorrow over the ways they've contributed to the mess in the world and their failure in trying to make things right. They see the selfish impulse at work in their hearts and come to realize they are part of the problem, not the solution. No matter how many times they've tried to do things right, or become a better person, or make the world a better place, they keep getting tripped up. They sense a moral standard outside of themselves that they constantly fall short of and feel that they've disappointed God and others. At some point, for many, a sense of despair sets in—the feeling that you can't escape your worst impulses, that no matter how many times you change your image or try to redesign and redefine your self, you run around in circles and never experience lasting change. Right then, once you get to the point where you realize you don't have anything to offer but empty hands, and once you look deep down into yourself and see cavern after cavern of competing desires, some of which lead you astray, you shrink back in sorrow for the ways you've hurt the people around you and the heart of God himself. And in the darkness of that grief, at the bottom of your sins and sadness, for the first time, you look *up*. In that supernatural flash, you are freed from the prison of your heart and your eyes are opened to see how God—the one who has every right to judge you for going your own way—has stretched out his arms to rescue you and bring you to the surface. What Jesus has done for you makes sense, and his unmistakable and beautiful love toward you makes all the difference. You stop looking in for salvation and start looking up.

In the "look in" approach to life, the word "faith" often gets reduced to a vague or sentimental feeling. We talk about "believing in yourself" or "having faith" that everything will work out, and we describe the religious or spiritual as "people of faith." But all of these phrases belong to the old paradigm where you look in before you look up. Faith becomes just a feeling, something that helps you through the day, and it's something you muster up from within yourself.

The Bible's understanding of faith is different. It refers to personal and total trust in God. The point isn't how much faith you have, but the person you have faith in. What matters isn't that you have a lot of faith, but that the one you're putting your faith in is worthy of it. That's what dependence looks like. You trust God with your life, and you trust him to bring you through death and into eternal bliss. The redesign described by the first followers of Jesus takes place when you come to the end of yourself, when you recognize there's no lasting hope in looking in, and so you turn from your old way of life, renounce your sins and failures, and turn your eyes toward Jesus as the one you love, the only one who can make you new. This is the great redesign—the moment of renewal. It happens in an instant, even if for some people, the steps are so subtle they may not know the exact moment the journey began. The effects of this redesign last a lifetime.

The letters near the end of the Bible describe the life of faith in terms of your "old self" and your "new self," implying that there's been a foundational and fundamental change in your orientation to life. You no longer look inside to find yourself and change yourself. You look up to God to determine your destiny. You look up to God in dependence and faith. You look up to God to see who you are meant to be. You look to God to discover how to live.

The Bible also describes this redesign in terms of "renewal of the mind."[69] It's *rethinking* yourself. You once considered yourself in a certain way, but now you consider yourself in a new way. Your identity has shifted. Your purpose in life, which was once all about pursuing whatever you desire the most in order to find happiness, is now about pursuing whatever *God* wants the most, because your desires have shifted and now better align with his. What you love has changed.

A New Display

How does the "look up" approach change the way we look around to others? Here is where we return to our primary purpose in life: we are created to be a display—a reflection—of God. All humans share the calling to reflect God, however much we fail at it because of the condition of sin. And all humans, because we are made in God's image, have innate dignity and worth. Yet because we are also fallen creatures, we deserve judgment. It is because we have a dignity that stands out from all the other creatures on earth that God takes our actions seriously and treats our behavior with moral significance.

After the great redesign takes place, the selfish impulse that would have us grasp for our own glory and make a display of ourselves begins to fade. We begin to display before the watching world what it means to live as God originally intended. With our sins forgiven, we are free to live differently. With judgment averted because of the cross, we are free to become merciful toward others. When we look around, we see ourselves as members of a family—a people we can dedicate ourselves to because together we are all dedicated to the God who rescued us.

Following Jesus is a lifelong journey of being gradually reshaped and molded into the image of the God who made us and saved us. We reflect God in how we relate to one another, in standing out from the world by the way in which we can forgive others when they do us wrong, or in how we love our enemies, or in how we deal with conflict as brothers and sisters who belong to the same family of God. We are free to bind ourselves in commitment to others because we have a God who has bound himself in commitment to us.

In the "look up" approach to life, when we look around, it's not so we can receive the old kind of affirmation, where people champion whatever path we've chosen. That kind of affirmation is superficial because it assumes that our identity and our actions are one and the same. Instead, we get a different kind of support. The people who belong to this family cheer on our baby steps of obedience, comfort us when we're discouraged, correct and guide us when we're in error, and train us for the challenges ahead. Here we find the beautiful combination of acceptance and aspiration that true friendship requires. Even as we are accepted because of what Jesus has done for us, we are challenged to aspire to a new way of life.

Over time we begin to display more and more the goodness and glory of God. When others see your life, they should recognize that you see God as your highest authority. They should see the diminishment of the selfish impulse. They should see you living in submission to King Jesus, who said others would know his followers by the way they love each other.[70] Loving others the way Jesus loves us is the path to a new kind of self-display, a freedom from self-centeredness, and an opportunity to think of others as more important than ourselves.[71]

You might think that a life that focuses on others, not yourself, would cause you to lose your own worth and individuality. But the truth is the opposite. You find yourself in giving yourself. The world gets bigger and seems grander. How suffocating and stifling to think that you can find your purpose by looking deep within your heart! Your heart is too small. How much better to go outside yourself, to greet the grandeur of the world with gratitude, to see everyone around you as someone made in God's image—people with their own hopes and fears, challenges and failures, sins and virtues—and to find a renewed purpose in serving them as Jesus has served you.

New Desires

What does the "look up" approach say about our desires? Here is where the project of rethinking our selves becomes challenging. Our hearts are full of conflicting desires, which is why the notion that you should just "follow your heart" doesn't make sense. But the Bible doesn't say we should never follow our hearts or pursue our desires; in fact, one of the psalms says that when we find our delight and joy in God, he will give us the desires of our heart.[72]

But notice how that promise connects delight and desire. You may be thinking that the point of religion is to repress your desires, to stifle your feelings, and to ignore your deepest longings. Unfortunately, some churches and religious institutions have given that impression. But rightly understood, following Jesus is not the destruction of desire, but the development of better desire. You won't change your life merely by repressing a desire, but by replacing it.

Rethinking yourself means you refuse to submit to the loudest desires of your heart, and that you recognize the need to find and develop new desires, new goals, and a new purpose in life.

Common sense says you should follow your heart. The Bible says you should direct your heart.[73] You point your heart in the way Jesus says you should go. There is a sense in which the survey statement we saw earlier, where most Americans believe happiness comes from "pursuing whatever we desire the most" is true. But only once our desires have been redirected. If God becomes our greatest and deepest desire, then yes, we will find happiness—foretastes of the richest joy in this life and then the feast of forever joy in the life to come.

The challenge is in directing our heart to God as our deepest desire. The replacement of lesser desires with greater ones, or bad desires with good ones, can feel a little like dying. You're embracing your true self, while disowning your fallen self. It's tough to die to old desires, or to stop old habits. It's hard to devote every part of your life to God: your finances, your relationships, your career, your sexuality, your spheres of authority, your hopes and dreams. It takes time. It's painful. Because we're conditioned to see our desires as a statement about our identity, it may feel like you're losing a central part of yourself, especially when we endure seasons of suffering. Hannah Anderson explains why:

> In moments of difficulty, confusion, and loss, God is stripping you of all the things you reach for instead of him. He is cutting and cleaning and crafting your life so it

can shine the light of his glory. Do not be afraid when this happens. . . . He is coming to reclaim his own, and he will not stop until you become your truest self.[74]

This is why we need faith. We trust that the calling of God to become who he has made us to be is infinitely better than anything we can dream of in this moment.

Imagine a mother and father adopting a little girl who has never lived anywhere but in the poverty of a tiny orphanage. Her new dad tells her he wants to clean her up, dress her as a princess, and take her to Disney World. When all she knows is the dirt of her present existence, and when she has grown accustomed to the lack of nutrition and the rotting smells, and when she has experienced only glimmers of joy here and there, she will have a hard time understanding the promise he's made to her. The question is: Will she step into that promise and adopt that identity? Will she leave the familiar surroundings to follow? He already sees her as a princess, riding on his shoulders and watching the fireworks. Can she see that future? Will she trust him? Will she leave behind the lesser things she loves in order to step into a new world where she will find better things to love?

This is what following Jesus is like. God looks at us and calls us his children. He knows the desires we have, some so deep we may remain unaware of them, and he sees us flailing about looking in all the wrong places to find satisfaction. He reaches out his hand and calls us to walk with him, trusting that the new desires he will give us will bring delight that far outweighs any of the old ones we put away. Faith means trusting God when he says our selfish desires lead to death, and taking his hand and stepping forward into the way of life.

New Definition

Now we arrive at the last D: definition. It may seem strange to only now talk about defining yourself, when the commonsense way of thinking about things makes looking inside to find and define yourself your starting point. But the "look up" approach to life puts self-definition last because it's not about discovering for yourself who you are, but discovering who God says you are. You look up to the one who made you, around to the family you now belong to, and then inside, finally, to see how God has defined you.

On the other side of the great redesign, God says you are his child, you belong to his family, you are no longer defined by your lesser desires or your past sins or your present struggles, but you have been washed clean by the death of Jesus on your behalf, and just as your sins have been counted as his, his goodness is now counted as yours. No longer are you on the road to judgment, but the path to life and joy and peace everlasting.

God your Father defines you as his adopted child, someone who is set apart from the rest of the world, someone who—as part of the community of faith—puts on display his goodness and glory. The fundamental reality that sets you apart is not something you find deep within your soul, but *someone* you know and love because he first loved you. The Bible describes this person as the Spirit of God himself, living within us, giving us the strength and the satisfaction of living according to his purposes. Your uniqueness doesn't come from who you are deep down inside, but in the grace of God given to you from outside.

This new definition brings not only the presence of God (through his Spirit) but also a renewed sense of purpose, a mission for your life. It's not about how you can further your name or your own personal agenda in life; it's about looking for ways to further the fame of King Jesus, to see more people come to know him and find their ultimate satisfaction in him, and to see the places where you have influence become a little more like the world should look when God is King.

This is the adventure of rethinking yourself in light of who Jesus is and what he has done for you. But you may be wondering about practical things we can do to keep from slipping back into old patterns of life? How do we keep looking up in a world where everyone else tells us to look in?

In the next chapter, we will look at practices and habits that will help us rebel against the commonsense view of our day by reminding us who we are, what defines us, how our desires are shaped, and what it means to display for others a life dedicated to the glory of God.

Reflection Questions

Which of the two dangers mentioned at the beginning of the chapter do you find more appealing—to see religion as a path to morality or as a path to inspiration? Why?

Have you experienced what is described here as the "new birth"? Do you know someone who claims they have experienced this?

What are some of the major differences between the "old self" and the "new self" as described by the Bible?

CHAPTER 11

Retraining Your Self

The irony of a book called *Rethink Your Self* is that you won't be able to truly rethink your self unless you do more than think.

The "look up" approach to life won't happen just because you think about your self differently. The transformation of your heart—the lifelong pursuit of happiness in God—only takes place when you *act* differently. Belief and behavior go together. Thinking and doing. Attitudes and actions.

Too often, people who attend church assume that merely believing the right truths will make them faithful. As long as you can check off a list of beliefs, as long as you *think* the right things, you're on the right track. But the Bible warns about those who turn their faith into something that only affects the head, and not the heart and hands. Faith without works is dead.[75] *Thinking* the right way only gets you so far.

Let's say you've recently been to the doctor, and you discover you need to lose some weight, cut back on red meat and sugar, and exercise more. You're in the "danger zone" health wise, and you need to make adjustments to your life if you want to improve your numbers before your next visit. Leaving the doctor's office, you've got new knowledge and understanding. You've received a diagnosis about your physical health. You begin to *rethink* yourself. Yes, you'd like to be healthy, and you'd like your desire for health to be stronger than your desire for red meat and sweets. What's more, you'd like to look your best by dropping twenty pounds, and you'd like to avoid a disease or a significant health challenge in the future. You know the problem, and you know the solution.

But is that enough? For most people, it's not. The big problem you'll face isn't a matter of knowledge, or of desire. The problem is your habits. You've gotten used to eating out and always going for the steak or hamburger. You've gotten into the habit of eating sugary snacks all day long at the office. You've stocked your pantry full of the food you love the most. You've gotten out of the habit of exercising regularly. Unless you change some of your habits, you're unlikely to see much change in your health, no matter how much knowledge and desire you have.

New habits must replace old habits. Instead of munching on jellybeans, you'll develop a taste for baby carrots. Instead of going right to the couch as soon as you get home from work, you'll get on your exercise bike. Instead of a pantry full of sugary cereals and snacks, you'll find healthier options to enjoy. Until you take steps to change your habits, you'll fail to see lasting change. Why? Because life transformation happens through discipline, not just through desire. Better put, it happens through the discipline *of* your desires.

Retraining Your Desires

You can read about the "look up" approach to life, nod along with everything I say, start to understand the difference between looking in and looking up, *and still go right back to the same patterns of life.* Rethinking your self will not suffice. You must also *retrain* your self.

In a letter to early followers of Jesus, Paul compared life to runners in a stadium who compete for a prize. The way you run the race of faith is through exercising "self-control in everything," he wrote. "I do not run like one who runs aimlessly or box like one beating the air. Instead, I discipline my body and bring it under strict control," he said.[76] Effort is indispensable to the life of following Jesus.

It's easy to read these words about effort and assume that faith is fundamentally about trying harder to change your life and your desires, all in your own power. But seeing effort in these terms would have us slip back into the old way of thinking where we look inside to muster up the power to change, rather than looking up to God for strength. The effort I am describing does not stand in opposition to, but is totally dependent on, God's grace and God's Spirit. The Bible tells you, paradoxically, to "work out your own salvation" for "it is God who is working in you both to will and to work according to his good purpose."[77]

So how do we adopt, practically, the "look up" approach to life, especially in a society that will constantly pull us in the direction of "looking in"? In other words, how do we resist the commonsense way of seeing the purpose of life and how can we counter our old way of thinking?

The answer is in reorganizing our lives around God and not ourselves. We don't just make room for God; we acknowledge it's his room, and his throne is at the center. And in order to do this, we'll need to replace some old habits with some new ones, and the good news is, with the help of God's Spirit and the encouragement of God's people, we know we're not alone.

The Necessity of the Community

Looking up instead of in will be nearly impossible unless you surround yourself with people who have the same outlook on life. We need the church. Mary Eberstadt says, "Trying to believe without a community of believers is like trying to work out a language for oneself."[78] But all too often, we adopt the commonsense view of looking in, which tells us we can go it alone.

Rethinking yourself requires rethinking the church. Research shows that many people who claim to be Christians do not see the church as essential or necessary for their spiritual well-being.[79] In other words, belonging to a community of faith is optional. If it helps you be a better person, then great! If it doesn't, that's fine, too.

But this way of thinking is steeped in the "look in" approach to life. It reduces the church to an add-on to your pursuit of your desires and your spiritual goals. It casts the church in the role of being your cheerleader when you need affirmation, when the priority is all in how you define yourself.

The Bible doesn't view the church this way. First and foremost, it's not about you at all. Gathering in worship with other believers is a way of pointing you and them, week after week, to God as the center and source of all things. Gathering in worship also reminds you of your membership in a family who will cheer you on when you are flagging and redirect you when you are wandering. If it's true that we become like what we worship, then we need the church to show us Jesus again and again, so that we slowly become more like him.

The church points you back to the redesign that began when you first stepped forward in faith, and the church also points you forward to the ultimate redesign that God has promised at the end of time. The church holds before you your past decision and your future destiny. In church, you celebrate the redesign of others as they pass through the waters of baptism. In church, you celebrate the broken body and shed blood of Jesus when you look around the table and, as a family, feast at his supper. Through the songs you sing, the sermons you hear, the Scriptures you read, you look around, and then together, you look up.

Unfortunately, it's easy for a church to become a "look in" type of place, much like other clubs and groups. We stay on the surface with our relationships, and hide our hypocrisies and struggles because we want our display to be acceptable to others. We slip into a paralyzing fear of failure, or find satisfaction by appearing superior to others, falling prey to a hyper-judgmental spirit. It doesn't take much for the church to become a bastion of self-righteousness or an enclave of shallow inspiration.

In order to resist these tendencies, you will need to forge deeper relationships, to the point you may be uncomfortable from time to time. The church is not a club you join, but a community you submit to. This means you will need to put aside your own preferences regarding your church. You will need to seek out people who come from different backgrounds and who have different interests, but who share with you the same story of grace and the same desire of looking up before looking in. You will also need to remember the mission of the church is bigger than your own personal project of bettering yourself. The church exists for the glory of God and the good of the world. We look up to God and then around to our neighbor—in order to show and share the love of Jesus.

A church deals with all sorts of temptations and sins, and you may in your discouragement decide you're better off without one. But abandoning the church says something untrue about what God is like. He has not abandoned you, no matter how flawed you remain. How then can we abandon the church with all her flaws? There is no perfect church and no perfect friend. Every church is a work in progress, and the same is true of you, too. The good news is that God is the one at work. Your church may be a far cry from the ideal, but you're better off looking for the signs of God at work there than by hopping around in search of a more spiritual place of service.

Commit to a Place

Speaking of church, we should also mention here the need for commitment in more general terms. As the "look in" approach to life has become common sense in our society, more and more people look for ways to show how free they are from previous generations, family constraints, or other outside forces. We are less connected to other people (part of the problem we saw earlier, when friendship equals shallow affirmation without truth-telling and commitment).

Commitment comes hard in a society where so many people see themselves as timeless and placeless. Timeless—you have no obligations to your forebears and little responsibility for future generations. Placeless—no roots can hold you down or put a claim on you when you have endless geographical choices. The result is a world in which we are unaware of our past and untethered to any particular place.

In a society that forgets its past and doesn't think much about its future, in which geographical heritage has little to no hold on a person, we often feel rootless and disoriented, as if we're just flitting through life with nothing to hold us down. At first, that sounds like freedom! In reality, that kind of life hinders us from commitments that bring lasting significance to our lives. Hannah Arendt once said,

> Without being bound to the fulfillment of promises, we would never be able to achieve the amount of identity and continuity which together produce a "person" about whom a story could be told; each of us would be condemned to wander helplessly and without direction in the darkness of his own lonely heart, caught in its ever-changing moods, contradictions, and equivocalities.[80]

We long for roots. It's no wonder, then, that websites and shows about finding your ancestors have grown in popularity in recent years. Despite the "look in" approach of discovering freedom by escaping obligations related to time or place, we are constantly drawn back to personal history and geography in hopes that tracing our roots through time and place will reveal the forces that have shaped the person we are called to "be true to" or to "find and express."

The "look up" approach to life calls for a commitment to God and to others, not just to whatever we think brings the most freedom to ourselves. You'll need to see yourself as rooted in time and place, oriented toward faith-forming practices that help you to maintain a sense of grounding in a fluid and fast-paced world. Maybe it will be through committing to a civic group, donating to a particular charity, advocating for justice, or volunteering your time with one organization over many years. Maybe it will be through your commitment to live in a particular town, even if you have opportunities to leave for a higher-paying job, because you feel a sense of responsibility for the community. Maybe it will be through ordering your time around ancient rhythms of worship, and by singing songs that remind you that you're only the latest in a long line of followers of Jesus who have sought to be faithful.

Rethinking and retraining yourself is a lifelong battle of putting others before yourself. God first, others second, you third. Look up, around, then in. The Brazilian theologian René Breuel explains it this way:

> To start with the self is to end with nothing
> but the self. But when we enter the rhythm

of life, the logic of the universe; when we step out of the selfish posture of sin and step into the dance of love, self-giving, and joy at the heart of reality; when we dare to live not for our own sake, but for others, like God does; when we look at life as a wondrous gift of grace that comes undeserved and unannounced, waiting to be received with humility; when we live as the loving creatures we were made to be, that's when happiness can arrive as God's gift to crown our holy living with delight.[81]

Looking up leads us to look around, and unless we commit to those around us, our heartfelt desires won't get reshaped in ways that challenge the selfish impulse. Commitment means that within your congregation and in your local community, you will look for tangible ways to serve, to put others before yourself. The habit of putting other people first won't come naturally, so you'll have to seek out situations where it's required. You'll need to serve in areas that do not seem so exciting. Find places that force you out of your comfort zone, look for needs that require attention, and then put yourself out there as a servant. Developing a servant's heart happens when, in light of the self-giving love of God, you roll up your sleeves and get your hands dirty on behalf of others.

Soak in the Story of the Bible

Another discipline to help you look up is Bible reading. Regular Bible reading means more than just mining the Bible for spiritual nuggets of inspiration that comfort you in the life you've already chosen for yourself. To read the Bible in a countercultural way means you seek to understand it on its own terms, to enter the world it describes and let it transform your way of thinking.

The most popular stories in our day often reinforce the narrative most common in our society: a main character reaches a crisis in self-understanding, faces obstacles and pushback from others, looks deep within to find the inner fortitude to keep going, and then overcomes the obstacles to reach their dreams and fulfill their destiny. That's the "look in" approach to life, and you see it romanticized over and over and over. A half-hour sermon once a week will not compete with hours of movies, TV shows, and songs that constantly reinforce the notion of *that* narrative.

In order to reorient yourself to God, you will need a regular regimen of reading the Bible. Perhaps you've tried different Bible reading plans before and failed.

Maybe you find the book too hard to understand. Or perhaps you gravitate toward the inspirational sections that just help you through your day. Don't be discouraged. Developing a hunger for the Bible may take some time. Like babies, we need bite-sized pieces at first, or help from someone who can cut up the meat so we can digest it. Like someone learning a new skill, we may need people and resources to explain parts of the Bible in a way we can understand. There's nothing embarrassing about starting out in your journey of reading the Bible. It's like learning to read all over again.

One reason some followers of Jesus start with a strong commitment to read the Bible and yet later run out of steam is that they have too high of an expectation of what they will *feel* every time they read. Christians believe the Bible is God's Word, and that he speaks to us through it. Yet so many times when we're reading the assigned portion of Scripture for the day, it all feels so, well, *ordinary*. We read a story, note a couple of interesting things, don't see how it applies to our lives today, and then move on. For example, by the time we near the end of the first books of the Bible, we've perused extensive instructions on how to build the tabernacle, learned how the sacrificial system is to be implemented, and endured a book of Numbers that is aptly titled. We may read the daily portion of Scripture, put down our pencil or highlighter and wonder, "Why don't I feel like my life is changing?"

If you feel this way, you're not alone. Of course, it's right for us to approach the Bible with anticipation, to expect to hear from God in a powerful and personal way. But the way the Bible does its work on our hearts is often not through the lightning bolt of inspiration, but through the gentle and quiet rhythms of daily submission, of opening up our lives before this open book and asking God to change us.

Change doesn't always happen overnight. Growth doesn't happen in an instant. Like other disciplines, improvement happens over time, as we eat and drink and exercise. The same is true of the spiritual sustenance we get through Scripture reading. Not every dinner takes place at a steak house. Not every meal is memorable. Can you remember what you had for lunch, say, two weeks ago? Probably not. But that meal sustained you, didn't it? In the same way, we come to feast on God's Word, recognizing that it's the daily rhythm of submitting ourselves to God and bringing our plans and hopes and fears to him that makes the difference.

There are times when God will speak to us like a thunderbolt, pressing something deep into our hearts. But it's not every day that you find something extraordinary that stays with you. Every day, though, in the ordinary routine of reading your Bible, you're still *eating*. You're coming to the table, asking the Lord to sustain you and nourish you through his Word. You're coming to the Gospels, looking at the story and teachings of Jesus again and again. Over time, the discipline of reading God's Word, hearing God's Word, discussing God's Word with other people in community—that has a profound effect on the kind of person you're becoming.

Praying and Fasting

As we consider ways of retraining our selves, two other disciplines bear mentioning: prayer and fasting. I've saved them for last because nothing seems more off-putting to most people than the idea that we'd spend a lot of time in prayer and fasting. Fasting means going without food, and we like food! Prayer doesn't come easily in a world filled with noise. But one of the ways we train our hearts is by disciplines that help to form our desires.

Fasting is a way of telling your body what your heart senses to be true: *I don't hunger for God enough, so I will deliberately go without food as a way of increasing my dependence on God when I am hungry.* Fasting is a response to an event that requires repentance and contrition, or a response to the recognition that your heart has grown flabby in its devotion to God.

Prayer is communion with God. Nothing is quite as common *and* strange as prayer. It's common because even people who say they don't believe in God still pray. (I believe the reason prayer is nearly universal is because we were created by a God who speaks, and so even those who don't acknowledge the presence or existence of a Creator still at some point find it almost impossible not to speak back to him.) It's strange because we are talking to an invisible being.

The temptation with prayer is similar to the other practices I've mentioned: you might turn this discipline into just another spiritual element to assist you in the way you want to live. The "look in" approach to life can easily incorporate prayer practices, mindfulness routines, meditation, breathing exercises, or solitude. But properly understood, prayer is not just another discipline that exists to bring peace to your life. The point of prayer is to orient you upward, not just inward. Yes, you'll discover things about yourself when you engage in the regular habit of praying, but the main purpose is not self-discovery; it's to know better the mind and heart of God. That's why, in Jesus' model prayer for his followers, he began by having us address God as our Father in heaven before asking that his name be known as holy, and that his kingdom would come and will be done on earth as in heaven.[82] In other words, *look up.*

There's no legalistic ritual of prayer that everyone has to adopt, but there's something to be said for certain traditions that have arisen over the years. Like kneeling. Why kneel? Because it is a posture of submission. Kneeling puts your body in a position that you want your heart to follow. Why lay prostrate on the ground from time to time when you pray? Because you can demonstrate with your body that you are fully submitted to God's will for your life. Why pray written prayers, like the psalms or the prayers from believers in past generations? Because, like a child learning to try on Daddy's shoes, your desires and words can be shaped by the Scriptures and by the people who have gone before you, who longed for God and loved him with all their hearts. Why pray at specific times of the day? Because these habits punctuate our daily routines with reminders that we live our lives before God, that the first thing we do in the morning is devote the day to him, and that we come to the table with gratitude for the gift of food, and that we go to bed with thanksgiving for another day of life. Why pray with other people? Because our prayers encourage one another and because we can affirm each other's prayers as we speak to God.

Prayer may be both common and strange, but rightly practiced it opens a window into the unseen realm where our Father is ready and willing to respond.

Replacing Habits

These are just a few of the most powerful habits you can put into practice in order to retrain your self and your desires. You may think: *I'm already so busy. I just don't have time.* You're probably right. If you're the type of person who runs from event to event, fills the day with activity that includes work, rest, eating, and entertainment, then yes, it's true; you likely don't have time to add new habits into your life. But there is still a way to make time for new habits, and it's through replacing some of your old habits.

Remember our response to the doctor's diagnosis? When you decide to eat healthier food, you aren't just adding some healthy options to all the bad things you've been eating, as if the way to change your life is to eat all the junk food you want as long as you finish it off with broccoli and cauliflower. No, eating healthy means *replacing* certain foods with others. It means retraining your appetite so that you no longer crave bad food and develop a taste for food that is better for you.

Who has more freedom? The person who abides by certain restrictions and enjoys healthier fare? Or the person who can't resist their appetites and eats whatever they want? We may be tempted, in a world that says the way to find happiness is to pursue whatever you desire the most, to say that the second person is freer than the first. They eat whatever they want! But there's a deeper vision of freedom at work in the other way of thinking, and it's the freedom to live according to a higher calling, the freedom to resist being enslaved to whatever your greatest desire or passion may be in the moment, the freedom to cultivate and experience better desires.

The power of a habit is that it eventually becomes like second nature to you. By removing the requirement to constantly make choices, you can settle into habits. For many people at night, watching a couple episodes of a popular drama is no longer a choice but a habit. You do it without thinking about it. We slip into habits everywhere in our lives, and these routines turn you into a certain kind of person, whether you realize it or not. If you can train yourself toward good habits, you don't have to rely solely on sheer willpower to try and do the right thing anymore.

If you make a habit of reading your Bible and praying every morning, without fail, over time you'll remove that choice and you'll have developed into the kind of person who, well, reads their Bible and prays every morning. If you make a habit of grabbing your phone first thing in the morning, checking the news headlines and responding to email, or playing a couple rounds of your favorite game, that habit will get harder and harder to break, and you'll develop into the kind of person who doesn't begin the day with any serious reflection on who you are and what you are called to become, but is addicted to distraction.

I'm not saying that it's morally wrong to do the latter, I'm just asking: which habit will help you become the kind of person who naturally looks *up* rather than *in*?

To be clear, plenty of people have kept a number of rituals and yet have seen their hearts grow cold to God. It's possible to adopt virtuous habits and *still* be a miserable person who has little love for God and neighbor. Even those who live in monasteries and pray multiple times a day are not immune to self-centeredness. Sin is insidious. It creeps into even the best of our efforts.

Changing your habits is not a surefire way to adopt the "look up" approach to life as you follow Jesus, but it is unlikely that you'll develop into someone who can rethink yourself without giving your habits some attention. Brushing your teeth twice a day and flossing every night may not keep you from getting the occasional cavity or chipped tooth, but you're more likely to be the kind of person with good oral hygiene if you develop those habits than if you don't.

So, take a good look at your life and consider the habits and disciplines you already have. You may not even think much about them. Do they point you to the "look in" approach or the "look up" approach? Are any of your habits or disciplines going to serve as barriers to the "look up" approach? Will they cause you to trip up and revert to the "look in" approach?

In order to rethink and retrain yourself, you must be intentional about the habits in your life. Look for ways to redirect your heart and your selfish desires so that through the practices of churchgoing, service, Bible reading, prayer and fasting you are able to subvert the commonsense wisdom of our day. These practices are not merely spiritual exercises, but acts of resistance in a world that will constantly point us back to ourselves.

Reflection Questions

What are some ways you've sought to retrain and discipline yourself in the past? What effect did your actions have?

Why is the community of faith so important for maintaining the "look up" approach to life?

"God first, others second, you third." What are some specific habits that would reinforce this priority in your life?

Conclusion

L ooking up is a lifelong journey. And I do mean *lifelong*. There are no shortcuts to becoming truer and truer to the self God has called you to be.

Some preachers or pastors offer something akin to a "get rich quick" scheme, except the promise is spiritual growth and the result is total fulfillment in the present (sometimes, the promise of actual wealth gets thrown into the mix). But the Bible doesn't teach us that happiness in its fullness will be ours in this life, or that the gradual growth of a believer into the image of Jesus will lead to a state of moral perfection. Sin remains present and continues to affect us.

Nothing I've said so far should imply that this journey is easy or that life transformation takes place in a moment. It takes courage and consistency to live according to this new identity that has been given to you. There will be stumbles and falls. You will take steps forward and back. Ironically, the more you understand God and his ways, the more likely you are to see remaining sins and stains in your life that you'd never noticed before.

But not for long. And not forever. The Bible promises that we will go through one more redesign. God promises that in the world he will remake at the end of time, when he judges all that is wrong with the world once and for all, when death is done and the forces of evil are forever vanquished, you are going to be perfect. You will become the most glorious version of yourself imaginable. You will be like Jesus more than ever, and yet you will still be *you* more than ever—the deepest possible version of *you*, the *you* that God always intended you to be. That is the vision of the future that should give you hope in the present.

Too many times, we think that the *real* you or the *real* me is the bumbling believer who can't get it right. We think we're authentic whenever we wallow in our struggles, and focus on what is still wrong with us, and fall prey to temptations that keep hounding us.

The Bible says the opposite. When you sin, you go against your newfound identity. You reject your new purpose. When you fall into temptation and disobey God, you're not being authentic, but *in*authentic to the person God has called you to be. He has issued his declaration over you. Whenever you sin, it's as if you're denying that declaration. Sin never makes you more human or more yourself; it always makes you less so. Once you've been through the first redesign (conversion) and once you've been promised the last redesign (at the end of time), every time you sin you are diminishing yourself. You are not being true to your new self. Once you are a follower of Jesus, you are most true to yourself when you are obeying Jesus and being conformed into his image.

So, don't look back; look forward. You are more likely to see success in the present when you have a vision of yourself in the future.[83] In other words, you're more likely to rethink your self when your goals are in line with whatever you believe your authentic self to be, and according to the Bible, your authentic self is your *future* state, not your past sins or present struggles. Living in light of the future is vital for following Jesus.

In *Mere Christianity*, C. S. Lewis explains the significant, lifetime impact of small, seemingly insignificant choices. He paints a picture of every human being on a trajectory toward the future, with victories and setbacks as part of our formation.

> Every time you make a choice you are turning the central part of you, the part

of you that chooses, into something a little different than it was before. And taking your life as a whole, with all your innumerable choices, all your life long you are slowly turning this central thing into a heavenly creature or a hellish creature: either into a creature that is in harmony with God, and with other creatures, and with itself, or else into one that is in a state of war and hatred with God, and with its fellow creatures, and with itself. To be the one kind of creature is heaven: that is, it is joy and peace and knowledge and power. To be the other means madness, horror, idiocy, rage, impotence, and eternal loneliness. Each of us at each moment is progressing to the one state or the other.[84]

With steps back and forward, with a strong sense of God's forgiveness and grace, relying on the Spirit as you seek deliverance from selfish desires, you grow into more and more of a warrior who is committed to the blazing purity of your new self and your reflection of God. You embrace the new identity God has given you, and even if you fall, you get back up and the battle goes on. Your eyes are not on the sins you've stumbled over in the past, but the Savior who cheers you on in the race. Your future self is not a shriveled soul limping through life, but a spiritually robust, shining force for goodness, filled with the grace and courage you need to fight against sin with every last ounce of your Spirit-given energy.

The promise of the Bible is that on the other side of death, when the resurrection power that was seen on Easter morning will be true of all God's people, we will be our truest and fullest selves. We will not disintegrate into the vast unknown. Nor will we unite with some cosmic force until our personalities are obliterated. We will be fully and totally ourselves, and at the same time more like Jesus than ever before.

Who will define us eternally? The God who made us and saved us. The "real you" is not the person who continually stumbles and falls in the pursuit of your dreams. The real you is when you look most like yourself *and* most like Jesus, when you are everything God made you to be. Like a king or queen who waits for the day of coronation, you are in a procession toward the moment when your head will wear a crown. You are defined by your future, not by your past.

On that day, your desires will be fully aligned. No longer will your heart feel the tug of competing desires. The mixed-up longings that today reveal the state of your heart in all of its muddledness will align to reveal the fulfillment of God's dream for your life. Your greatest delight will come from knowing and loving God, your greatest desire. God will be yours, and you will be his, forever.

On that day, you will take your place alongside everyone else who knows and loves God—each person magnificent in their uniqueness and individuality, yet lifting their voice to join the chorus of praise to Jesus, so that every voice, beautiful in its uniqueness, serves to blend into the beauty of the whole. Relationships will be marked by harmony, not division. The world will know peace, not conflict. Your heart will feel joy, not sadness. With all of your fallenness burned away like dross, your heart will be pure gold, and you will forever be a perfect display of the majesty and love of the God who made you.

So whenever you hear the commonsense wisdom of the world telling you to chase your dreams and follow your heart, telling you that you are enough and should be true to yourself, remember the greater adventure: to be true to your *future* self, to know that you aren't enough, but Jesus is, to follow the heart of God, and to chase the dream he has for the world.

Acknowledgments

I t would be ironic if in writing this book I had begun by looking in, to see how I might express myself through this work. Instead, with gratitude, I can trace the roots of this book back to my childhood, to the moment when King Jesus lifted my head and my eyes caught his for the first time. I am grateful to my parents, my brothers and sister, and the church families I've belonged to over the years for how they have continually directed my gaze upward. My desire is that the writing here would reflect the wisdom and glory and love of Jesus, so that many more will experience the power of looking up before looking in.

I also appreciate the friends and colleagues who pressed me to write an easy-to-understand book on a topic with profound philosophical implications. I took the opportunity to "look around," and I received constant encouragement as well as constructive criticism from those who agreed to review this manuscript and offer suggestions: Collin Hansen, Ivan Mesa, Art and Ashlee Ocegueda, Wade Urig, Thien-Y Bonesteele, Greg Breazeale, Matt Smethurst, Chris Martin, Ashley Unzicker, Mary Wiley, Chris and Alex Windings, and Bill Noe. I'm grateful for the editorial oversight provided by Taylor Combs. Were I to add to the list everyone with whom I've had good conversation about expressive individualism over the years—including Tim Keller, my colleagues at LifeWay, Alan Noble, Mike Cosper, professors at Southeastern Seminary, and some of my students at Wheaton College—these acknowledgments would extend into several pages.

Most of all, I am grateful to my wife, Corina, for her unfailing support of me in my calling as a writer, as well as to our kids who are quickly growing up—Timothy, Julia, and David. My prayer for them is the prayer I offer for all who read this book: *May you be renewed in knowledge according to the image of your Creator* (Col. 3:10).

Notes

1. See Christian Smith and Melina Lundquist Denton's analysis of survey results in *Soul Searching: The Religious and Spiritual Lives of American Teenagers* (Oxford University Press, 2009). See also Christian Smith and Patricia Snell, *Souls in Transition: The Religious and Spiritual Lives of Emerging Adults* (Oxford University Press, 2009); Robert Wuthnow, *After the Baby Boomers: How Twenty- and Thirty-Somethings Are Shaping the Future of American Religion* (Princeton University Press, 2010); Tim Clydesdale and Kathleen Garces-Foley, *The Twenty-Something Soul: Understanding the Religious and Secular Lives of American Young Adults* (Oxford University Press, 2019); and David Kinnaman and Gabe Lyons, *Good Faith: Being a Christian When Society Thinks You're Irrelevant and Extreme* (Grand Rapids: Baker Books, 2016).

2. For an academic analysis of this view of the world from a number of sociologists and scholars, see Robert Bellah, Richard Madsen, William Sullivan, Ann Swidler, Steven Tipton, *Habits of the Heart: Individualism and Commitment in American Life* (University of California Press, 2017). They use the term "expressive individualism" to describe this approach to life. Yuval Levin defines expressive individualism this way: "That

term suggests not only a desire to pursue one's own path but also a yearning for fulfillment through the definition and articulation of one's own identity. It is a drive both to be more like whatever you already are and also to live in society by fully asserting who you are. The capacity of individuals to define the terms of their own existence by defining their personal identities is increasingly equated with liberty and with the meaning of some of our basic rights, and it is given pride of place in our self-understanding." Yuval Levin, *The Fractured Republic: Renewing America's Social Contract in the Age of Individualism* (New York: Basic Books, 2017), 148. There's a similar definition given by the philosopher Charles Taylor who uses "the age of authenticity" as a descriptor. We could define "authenticity" in different ways. When we're talking about "authenticity" as the opposite of "hypocrisy," then striving for authenticity becomes a good thing.

But Taylor does not use "authenticity" as a synonym for integrity or honesty. He uses the term in a way that pits *authenticity* against *conformity*. Here's Taylor's definition: "I mean the understanding of life which emerges with the Romantic expressivism of the late-eighteenth century, that each one of us has his/her own way of realizing our humanity, and that it is important to find and live out one's own, as against surrendering to conformity with a model imposed on us from outside, by society, or the previous generation, or religious or political authority." Charles Taylor, *A Secular Age* (Harvard University Press, 2009), 475. The key here is that the purpose of life is to find one's deepest self and then express that to the world, forging that identity in ways that counter whatever family, friends, political affiliations, previous generations, or religious authorities might say. (In case you wonder what this looks like in pop culture, just think of the many Disney movies that follow a narrative plot line of someone finding and forging their self-identity in opposition to the naysayers!)

3. David Kinnaman and Gabe Lyons, *Good Faith: Being a Christian When Society Thinks You're Irrelevant and Extreme* (Grand Rapids: Baker Books, 2016), 58.

4. Ibid.

5. Gregory of Nyssa, *From Glory to Glory*, ed. Jean Danielou (Crestwood, NY: St. Vladimir's Press, 1961), 87–88.

6. Jeffrey Arnett, quoted by Jean M. Twenge, *Generation Me: Why Today's Young Americans Are More Confident, Assertive, Entitled—and More Miserable Than Ever Before* (New York: Free Press, 2006), 83.

7. David Brooks, *The Second Mountain* (New York: Random House, 2019), 18.

8. For example, Stephen Colbert's address at Wake Forest University in 2015 ended with an encouragement to students to "find the courage to decide for yourself what is right and what is wrong" and then to "make the world good according to your standards," no matter what others might think. Colbert's intention is noble. He wants to encourage the graduates not to throw in the towel when things get tough. He doesn't want them to define themselves by what their critics say. For Colbert, the way to avoid a feeling of failure is to create your own test and then grade it yourself. Why worry about passing a test that someone else has created for you? Why feel bad for failing to meet some externally imposed standard? The problem with Colbert's advice is that it doesn't eradicate the feeling of failure or the angst of despair; it just moves it back a level. With no

outside reference, with no ideal outside of your own mind and your own experiences, you will constantly wonder: *Are my standards right? Did I create a test that is objectively good? Did I shoot high enough?* You won't worry about other people judging your performance, but you'll *always* wonder about your self-created standard of judgment for that performance. https://time.com/3883513/stephen-colbert-graduation-speech-wfu/

9. This tension is expressed in the song Kelly Clarkson sings at the end of the animated film *Ugly Dolls.* In "Broken and Beautiful," she declares in the first verse her independence from everyone else and asserts her self-sufficiency, but then the mood changes and her words tumble out as a heartfelt plea to be held by someone who won't try to "fix" her or "change a thing." The song finishes as an anthem that declares she is "broken" and "it's beautiful."

10. According to Jonathan Haidt and Greg Lukianoff's book, *The Coddling of the American Mind: How Good Intentions and Bad Ideas Are Setting Up a Generation for Failure* (New York: Penguin Press, 2018), three "Great Untruths" are responsible for many of the problems we face in certain segments of American society: The Untruth of Fragility (What doesn't kill you makes you weaker), The Untruth of Emotional Reasoning (Always trust your feelings), The Untruth of Us vs Them (Life is a battle between good people and evil people). *The Coddling of the American Mind* defines these untruths, provides examples of how these beliefs affect our society, traces the historical path to show how we arrived at this cultural moment, and then makes a case for how we can re-embrace wisdom as we engage in public life. Because the authors have expertise in different fields (Haidt in social psychology and Lukianoff in law), they

mount a multidimensional offensive against the Untruths. They show how these pernicious ideas contradict ancient wisdom and modern psychological research on well-being, and lead to harmful consequences for the individuals and communities who embrace them.

11. Heather Havrilesky, "It's Never Been Harder to Be Young," *New York Magazine* (July 11, 2016); https://www.thecut.com/2016/07/ask-polly-advice-lessons.html.

12. Tim Keller makes the point that modern notions of identity are illusory. He writes: "We can't say to ourselves, 'I don't care that literally everyone else in the world thinks I'm a monster. I love myself and that is all that matters.' That would not convince us of our worth, unless we are mentally unsound. We need someone from outside to say we are of great worth, and the greater the worth of that someone or someones, the more power they have to instill a sense of self and of worth. Only if we are approved and loved by someone whom we esteem can we achieve any self-esteem." *Making Sense of God: Finding God in the Modern World* (New York: Viking, 2016), 125.

13. Michelle Boorstein reports on this phenomenon in the *Washington Post*, "Some nonbelievers still find solace in prayer," June 24, 2013; https://www.washingtonpost.com/local/non-believers-say-their-prayers-to-no-one/2013/06/24/b7c8cf50-d915-11e2-a9f2-42ee3912ae0e_story.html.

14. This mix of "looking up" as another way of "looking in" shows up in strange places. Consider the theme song from the children's animated Christmas film, *The Star*, sung by Mariah Carey: "The Star." The first verse tells us to look up to the sky, to "follow the light" and let "the Lord" be our guide. But then the chorus adds "follow your heart" alongside the

admonition to "follow the star," no matter what anyone says or does to oppose you. By the end of the song, one refrain is chanted again and again: "Follow your heart; it's Christmas." The lyrics encapsulate the approach that would have us "look up" as a way of appropriating spiritual guidance and support for what is really just another way of "looking in."

15. The Bible has many statements that express sentiments such as the one found in the prayer of Psalm 16:11: "You reveal the path of life to me; in your presence is abundant joy; at your right hand are eternal pleasures."

16. Genesis 1:1: "In the beginning God created the heavens and the earth."

17. In the Bible, God first reveals his name to Moses, the leader he raised up to deliver the people of Israel from slavery in Egypt. Exodus 3:13–15: "Then Moses asked God, 'If I go to the Israelites and say to them, "The God of your ancestors has sent me to you," and they ask me, "What is his name?" what should I tell them?' God replied to Moses, 'I AM WHO I AM. This is what you are to say to the Israelites: I AM has sent me to you.' God also said to Moses, 'Say this to the Israelites: The LORD, the God of your ancestors, the God of Abraham, the God of Isaac, and the God of Jacob, has sent me to you. This is my name forever; this is how I am to be remembered in every generation.'"

18. In her book on the crucifixion, theologian Fleming Rutledge describes how Sin in the letters of the apostle Paul is described as a power, a "malign force over which the unaided human being has no control. . . . Sin is a *verb*, something people perform or engage in (Rom. 3:23). Sin is a *dominion* under which humanity exists (Rom. 3:9)." *The Crucifixion:*

Understanding the Death of Jesus Christ (Grand Rapids: William B. Eerdmans, 2015), 189.

19. https://www.pewresearch.org/fact-tank/2018/04/25/key-findings-about-americans-belief-in-god/

20. See Christian Smith and Melina Lundquist Denton's analysis of survey results in *Soul Searching: The Religious and Spiritual Lives of American Teenagers* (Oxford University Press, 2009). See also the number of churchgoing Christians who see God more in terms of a spiritual force of some sort, rather than in personal terms. Tim Clydesdale and Kathleen Garces-Foley, *The Twenty-Something Soul: Understanding the Religious and Secular Lives of American Young Adults* (Oxford University Press, 2019).

21. Gretchen Rubin, *The Happiness Project* (New York: Harper, 2011), 4, 10, 72.

22. Philosopher James K. A. Smith writes, "To be human is to be on a quest. To live is to be embarked on a kind of unconscious journey toward a destination of your dreams." *You Are What You Love: The Spiritual Power of Habit* (Grand Rapids: Brazos Press, 2016), 10.

23. The seventeenth-century philosopher Blaise Pascal recognized this problem well before the arrival of social media. In his *Pensées* (#806), he wrote: "We are not satisfied with the life we have in ourselves and our own being. We want to lead an imaginary life in the eyes of others, and so we try to make an impression. We strive constantly to embellish and preserve our imaginary being, and neglect the real one." Quoted in Peter Kreeft, *Christianity for Modern Pagans: Pascal's Pensées Edited, Outlined, and Explained* (San Francisco: Ignatius Press, 1993), 79.

24. Matthew 22:35–40 records this conversation between Jesus and an expert in the Jewish law. "And one of them, an expert in the law, asked a question to test him: 'Teacher, which command in the law is the greatest?' He said to him, 'Love the Lord your God with all your heart, with all your soul, and with all your mind. This is the greatest and most important command. The second is like it: Love your neighbor as yourself. All the Law and the Prophets depend on these two commands.'"

25. The reflections of this man, traditionally ascribed to King Solomon, who calls himself "The Teacher," are found in the book Ecclesiastes.

26. The promises made to Abraham are found in Genesis 12, 15, and 17.

27. Genesis 32

28. Exodus 20; Deuteronomy 5

29. The heart of God expressed through the prophetic writings often sounds like this plea, recorded in Joel 2:12–13. "Even now—this is the LORD's declaration—turn to me with all your heart, with fasting, weeping, and mourning. Tear your hearts, not just your clothes, and return to the LORD your God. For he is gracious and compassionate, slow to anger, abounding in faithful love, and he relents from sending disaster." The prophets portray God as all-powerful and holy, while also giving voice to God's passionate desire to see his people return to him, as if he were a spurned lover.

30. The books of Ezra and Nehemiah record this return to the land.

31. Mark 1:15

32. Matthew 5:1–12

33. Matthew 10:39

34. Mark 8:36–37

35. Mark 7:15

36. Luke 6:45

37. Mark 8:34; 10:29–31

38. Luke 14:26

39. Luke 9:23

40. John Stott, *Christ the Cornerstone: Collected Essays of John Stott* (Bellingham, WA: Lexham Press, 2019), 70.

41. Matthew 6:1: "Be careful not to practice your righteousness in front of others to be seen by them. Otherwise, you have no reward with your Father in heaven."

42. Matthew 5:14–16: "You are the light of the world. A city situated on a hill cannot be hidden. No one lights a lamp and puts it under a basket, but rather on a lampstand, and it gives light for all who are in the house. In the same way, let your light shine before others, so that they may see your good works and give glory to your Father in heaven."

43. Matthew 6:2–6, 16–18: "So whenever you give to the poor, don't sound a trumpet before you, as the hypocrites do in the synagogues and on the streets, to be applauded by people. Truly I tell you, they have their reward. But when you give to the poor, don't let your left hand know what your right hand is doing, so that your giving may be in secret. And your Father who sees in secret will reward you. Whenever you pray, you must not be like the hypocrites, because they love to pray standing in the synagogues and on the street corners to be seen by people. Truly I tell you, they have their reward. But when you pray, go into your private room, shut your door, and pray to your Father who is in secret. And your Father who sees in secret will reward you. . . . Whenever you fast, don't be gloomy like

the hypocrites. For they disfigure their faces so that their fasting is obvious to people. Truly I tell you, they have their reward. But when you fast, put oil on your head and wash your face, so that your fasting isn't obvious to others but to your Father who is in secret. And your Father who sees in secret will reward you."

44. In a secular age, many readers of the Gospels may be taken aback by how forthrightly and without any reservation the writers talk about evil spirits or demons. You may be inclined to think of evil spirits as belonging to the category of ghosts or haunts or UFOs. We tend to attribute the bad behavior of humans to a problematic past, or to misunderstanding, or to a lack of education. Perhaps you read accounts of exorcism and find them farfetched. At the same time, although you see yourself as educated and scientific, you believe it good to remain open-minded and inclusive of other cultural traditions. If you value diversity and multiculturalism, you should be open to the perspectives of people in other parts of the world. Takatemjen, a Christian writer in South Asia, says this: "Westerners tend to be embarrassed by accounts of demon possession and miraculous healings, for such things do not fit into their worldview. Not so in South Asia. Here people accept that demonic forces can affect people." *South Asia Bible Commentary: A One Volume Commentary on the Whole Bible* (Open Door Publications: Rajasthan, India, 2015), 1343. We would do well to realize that there are certain cases, even here in the West, where all our secular theories and psychological explanations fall short. When brought face to face with evil actions or desires beyond rational explanation, even those who deny the existence of the supernatural find themselves turning to words like "evil" and "depraved" and "demons."

45. John 8:54–59: "'If I glorify myself,' Jesus answered, 'my glory is nothing. My Father—about whom you say, "He is our God"—he is the one who glorifies me. You do not know him, but I know him. If I were to say I don't know him, I would be a liar like you. But I do know him, and I keep his word. Your father Abraham rejoiced to see my day; he saw it and was glad.' The Jews replied, 'You aren't fifty years old yet, and you've seen Abraham?' Jesus said to them, 'Truly I tell you, before Abraham was, I am.' So they picked up stones to throw at him. But Jesus was hidden and went out of the temple."

46. Mark 2:1–12: "When he entered Capernaum again after some days, it was reported that he was at home. So many people gathered together that there was no more room, not even in the doorway, and he was speaking the word to them. They came to him bringing a paralytic, carried by four of them. Since they were not able to bring him to Jesus because of the crowd, they removed the roof above him, and after digging through it, they lowered the mat on which the paralytic was lying. Seeing their faith, Jesus told the paralytic, 'Son, your sins are forgiven.' But some of the scribes were sitting there, questioning in their hearts: 'Why does he speak like this? He's blaspheming! Who can forgive sins but God alone?' Right away Jesus perceived in his spirit that they were thinking like this within themselves and said to them, 'Why are you thinking these things in your hearts? Which is easier: to say to the paralytic, "Your sins are forgiven," or to say, "Get up, take your mat, and walk"? But so that you may know that the Son of Man has authority on earth to forgive sins'—he told the paralytic—'I tell you: get up, take your mat, and go home.'

Immediately he got up, took the mat, and went out in front of everyone. As a result, they were all astounded and gave glory to God, saying, 'We have never seen anything like this!'"

47. John 10:23–33: "Jesus was walking in the temple in Solomon's Colonnade. The Jews surrounded him and asked, 'How long are you going to keep us in suspense? If you are the Messiah, tell us plainly.' 'I did tell you and you don't believe,' Jesus answered them. 'The works that I do in my Father's name testify about me. But you don't believe because you are not of my sheep. My sheep hear my voice, I know them, and they follow me. I give them eternal life, and they will never perish. No one will snatch them out of my hand. My Father, who has given them to me, is greater than all. No one is able to snatch them out of the Father's hand. I and the Father are one.' Again the Jews picked up rocks to stone him. Jesus replied, 'I have shown you many good works from the Father. For which of these works are you stoning me?' 'We aren't stoning you for a good work,' the Jews answered, 'but for blasphemy, because you—being a man—make yourself God.'"

48. Luke 7:34

49. Matthew 9:10–13: "While he was reclining at the table in the house, many tax collectors and sinners came to eat with Jesus and his disciples. When the Pharisees saw this, they asked his disciples, 'Why does your teacher eat with tax collectors and sinners?' Now when he heard this, he said, 'It is not those who are well who need a doctor, but those who are sick. Go and learn what this means: I desire mercy and not sacrifice. For I didn't come to call the righteous, but sinners.'"

50. John 14:6: "Jesus told him, 'I am the way, the truth, and the life. No one comes to the Father except through me.'"

51. Matthew 7:13–14: "Enter through the narrow gate. For the gate is wide and the road broad that leads to destruction, and there are many who go through it. How narrow is the gate and difficult the road that leads to life, and few find it."

52. Matthew 5:17–20: "Don't think that I came to abolish the Law or the Prophets. I did not come to abolish but to fulfill. For truly I tell you, until heaven and earth pass away, not the smallest letter or one stroke of a letter will pass away from the law until all things are accomplished. Therefore, whoever breaks one of the least of these commands and teaches others to do the same will be called least in the kingdom of heaven. But whoever does and teaches these commands will be called great in the kingdom of heaven. For I tell you, unless your righteousness surpasses that of the scribes and Pharisees, you will never get into the kingdom of heaven."

53. Jean Twenge, *iGen: Why Today's Super-Connected Kids Are Growing Up Less Rebellious, More Tolerant, Less Happy—and Completely Unprepared for Adulthood—and What That Means for the Rest of Us* (New York: Atria Books, 2017).

54. Psalm 96:10–13 expresses this sentiment well. "'The LORD reigns. The world is firmly established; it cannot be shaken. He judges the peoples fairly.' Let the heavens be glad and the earth rejoice; let the sea and all that fills it resound. Let the fields and everything in them celebrate. Then all the trees of the forest will shout for joy before the LORD, for he is coming—for he is coming to judge the earth. He will judge the world with righteousness and the peoples with his faithfulness."

55. I've seen several people use the phrase "hinge of history" to describe the events at the heart of the gospel, but

my friend Mike Cosper once used it to describe Christmas, and
it has stuck with me ever since. https://www.thegospelcoalition
.org/article/christmas-the-hinge-of-history/

56. Leviticus, which lays out the elaborate instructions
surrounding the different kinds of sacrifices and their purposes,
is one of the primary sources in the Bible for understanding the
significance of the atonement.

57. Mark 12:17

58. Matthew 5:38–48: "You have heard that it was said,
'An eye for an eye and a tooth for a tooth.' But I tell you, don't
resist an evildoer. On the contrary, if anyone slaps you on your
right cheek, turn the other to him also. As for the one who
wants to sue you and take away your shirt, let him have your
coat as well. And if anyone forces you to go one mile, go with
him two. Give to the one who asks you, and don't turn away
from the one who wants to borrow from you. You have heard
that it was said, Love your neighbor and hate your enemy. But
I tell you, love your enemies and pray for those who persecute
you, so that you may be children of your Father in heaven. For
he causes his sun to rise on the evil and the good, and sends
rain on the righteous and the unrighteous. For if you love those
who love you, what reward will you have? Don't even the tax
collectors do the same? And if you greet only your brothers and
sisters, what are you doing out of the ordinary? Don't even the
Gentiles do the same? Be perfect, therefore, as your heavenly
Father is perfect."

59. The crucifixion narratives are found in Matthew 26–27;
Mark 14–15, Luke 22–23, and John 18–19.

60. Mark 8:31–33; 9:30–32; 10:32–34

61. Mark 14:32–36: "Then they came to a place named Gethsemane, and he told his disciples, 'Sit here while I pray.' He took Peter, James, and John with him, and he began to be deeply distressed and troubled. He said to them, 'I am deeply grieved to the point of death. Remain here and stay awake.' He went a little farther, fell to the ground, and prayed that if it were possible, the hour might pass from him. And he said, '*Abba*, Father! All things are possible for you. Take this cup away from me. Nevertheless, not what I will, but what you will.'"

62. Sarah Ruden, *The Face of Water: A Translator on Beauty and Meaning in the Bible* (New York: Pantheon, 2017), 46.

63. N. T. Wright's *The Resurrection of the Son of God* (*Christian Origins and the Question of God,* Volume 3) (Minneapolis: Fortress Press, 2003) examines the biblical texts in light of ancient pagan and Jewish thought regarding life after death, as opposed to resurrection (life *after* life after death).

64. One of Jesus' better-known disciples, for example, Peter, described Jesus' death by alluding to and quoting from ancient Scriptures: "He did not commit sin, and no deceit was found in his mouth; when he was insulted, he did not insult in return; when he suffered, he did not threaten but entrusted himself to the one who judges justly. He himself bore our sins in his body on the tree; so that, having died to sins, we might live for righteousness. By his wounds you have been healed. For you were like sheep going astray, but you have now returned to the Shepherd and Overseer of your souls" (1 Pet. 2:22–25).

65. Romans 1:1–6: "Paul, a servant of Christ Jesus, called as an apostle and set apart for the gospel of God—which he promised beforehand through his prophets in the Holy

Scriptures—concerning his Son, Jesus Christ our Lord, who was a descendant of David according to the flesh and was appointed to be the powerful Son of God according to the Spirit of holiness by the resurrection of the dead. Through him we have received grace and apostleship to bring about the obedience of faith for the sake of his name among all the Gentiles, including you who are also called by Jesus Christ."

66. See the entire first chapter of Paul's letter to the Ephesians.

67. Paul's dismay is recorded in Galatians 1.

68. John 3:1–8: "There was a man from the Pharisees named Nicodemus, a ruler of the Jews. This man came to him at night and said, 'Rabbi, we know that you are a teacher who has come from God, for no one could perform these signs you do unless God were with him.' Jesus replied, 'Truly I tell you, unless someone is born again, he cannot see the kingdom of God.' 'How can anyone be born when he is old?' Nicodemus asked him. 'Can he enter his mother's womb a second time and be born?' Jesus answered, 'Truly I tell you, unless someone is born of water and the Spirit, he cannot enter the kingdom of God. Whatever is born of the flesh is flesh, and whatever is born of the Spirit is spirit. Do not be amazed that I told you that you must be born again. The wind blows where it pleases, and you hear its sound, but you don't know where it comes from or where it is going. So it is with everyone born of the Spirit.'"

69. Romans 12:1–2: "Therefore, brothers and sisters, in view of the mercies of God, I urge you to present your bodies as a living sacrifice, holy and pleasing to God; this is your true worship. Do not be conformed to this age, but be transformed

by the renewing of your mind, so that you may discern what is the good, pleasing, and perfect will of God."

70. John 13:35

71. Philippians 2:3–4: "Do nothing out of selfish ambition or conceit, but in humility consider others as more important than yourselves. Everyone should look not to his own interests, but rather to the interests of others."

72. Psalm 37:4: "Take delight in the LORD, and he will give you your heart's desires."

73. I'm indebted to my editor, Taylor Combs, for this insight, a variation of which he heard from his pastor, Scott Patty.

74. Hannah Anderson, "Reflection: Made in God's Image," in Melissa Kruger, editor, *Identity Theft: Reclaiming the Truth of Who We Are in Christ* (Deerfield, IL: The Gospel Coalition, 2018), 26.

75. James 2:14–26: "What good is it, my brothers and sisters, if someone claims to have faith but does not have works? Can such faith save him? If a brother or sister is without clothes and lacks daily food and one of you says to them, 'Go in peace, stay warm, and be well fed,' but you don't give them what the body needs, what good is it? In the same way faith, if it doesn't have works, is dead by itself. But someone will say, 'You have faith, and I have works.' Show me your faith without works, and I will show you faith by my works. You believe that God is one. Good! Even the demons believe—and they shudder. Senseless person! Are you willing to learn that faith without works is useless? Wasn't Abraham our father justified by works in offering Isaac his son on the altar? You see that faith was active together with his works, and by works, faith was made

complete, and the Scripture was fulfilled that says, Abraham believed God, and it was credited to him as righteousness, and he was called God's friend. You see that a person is justified by works and not by faith alone. In the same way, wasn't Rahab the prostitute also justified by works in receiving the messengers and sending them out by a different route? For just as the body without the spirit is dead, so also faith without works is dead."

76. 1 Corinthians 9:24–27

77. Philippians 2:12–13

78. Mary Eberstadt, "How the West Really Lost God," June 1, 2007; https://www.hoover.org/research/how-west-really-lost-god.

79. See the Pew Forum survey on "religion in everyday life," April 12, 2016, https://www.pewforum.org/2016/04/12/religion-in-everyday-life/.

80. Hannah Arendt, quoted in David Brooks's *The Second Mountain*, 57.

81. René Breuel, *The Paradox of Happiness: Finding True Joy in a World of Counterfeits* (Bellingham, WA: Kirdale Press, 2018), 45.

82. Matthew 6:9–13 records what is often called "The Lord's Prayer," which is Jesus' instruction on what and how to pray. "Therefore, you should pray like this: Our Father in heaven, your name be honored as holy. Your kingdom come. Your will be done on earth as it is in heaven. Give us today our daily bread. And forgive us our debts, as we also have forgiven our debtors. And do not bring us into temptation, but deliver us from the evil one."

83. Not long ago, researchers conducted several studies to see what matters most when trying to achieve a goal. What they

found was this: "The more closely a goal aligned with a person's sense of self—what the researchers call *goal authenticity*—the greater the progress. . . . Subjects indicated their progress toward goals that made them 'feel like they are really being themselves' . . . [or] 'reflects who I am deep down inside.' People made greater progress toward more-authentic goals." *Harvard Business Review*, July–August 2019.

84. C. S. Lewis, *Mere Christianity* (1952; repr., New York: HarperOne, 2015), 92.

also available from
TREVIN WAX

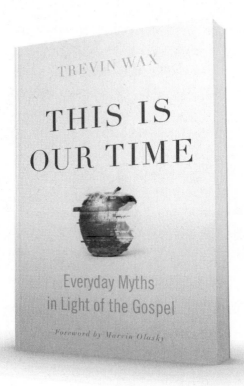

"No one combines gospel depth, keen insight, practical help and good storytelling like Trevin Wax. This book is good on every level."

- pastor and author *J.D. Greear*

In *This Is Our Time*, Trevin Wax provides snapshots of twenty-first-century American Life in order to help Christians understand the times. By analyzing our common beliefs and practices (smartphone habits, entertainment intake, and our views of shopping, sex, marriage, politics, and life's purpose), Trevin helps us see through the myths of society to the hope of the gospel.

AVAILABLE WHEREVER BOOKS ARE SOLD